Planning Learning Resource Centres in Schools and Colleges

Rosemary Raddon

Gower   A Grafton Book

Published by
Gower Publishing Company Limited
Gower House, Croft Road
Aldershot, Hants GU11 3HR

British Library Cataloguing in Publication Data

Raddon, Rosemary
   Planning learning resource centres in schools and
   colleges.
   1. Teaching aids and devices
   I. Title
   371.3'078   LB1043

ISBN 0–566–03435–2

Planning Learning Resource Centres in Schools and Colleges

Certainly it is harde to playse everyman because of dyversite and chaunge of language. For in these days everyman that is in any reputacyon in his countrie, wyll utter his communycacyon and matters in such manners and termes that fewe men shall understande theym.

William Caxton

Contents

Diagrams

Acknowledgements

I would like to thank my friends Ivy Davies and
Elaine Perra who helped to make this book possible.
Ivy typed the manuscript in her inimitable way, and
Elaine helped design the diagrams. Any mistakes
are mine and not theirs.

Drawings and photographs are reproduced by courtesy of the Greater
London Council Department of Architecture and Civic Design

Introduction

The planning and the use of services and facilities in a time of financial constraint becomes increasingly important in order to maintain a balance of provision. A resource centre supports the institution within which it is placed, and the institution in turn supports it, and the interaction, amoeba-like, never ceases. This crucial interaction of resources, in the widest sense, supports and complements the policy of the establishment and the needs of learners and teachers at all levels. The total integration between policies, planning, plans, structures, services and their evaluation, so that each is seen as part of the whole, while independent in itself, is part of a systematic approach to the service, ensuring an effective relationship between each part and the whole, and each part and other parts of the system.

Local policies are determined and constrained by many forces, including the external ones of power politics, finance, economic problems, national education and training policies, social changes, educational changes (particularly in the implementation of new curricula) and research. If an institution is an 'environment for learning', then it must be concerned with the planned use of resources as part of its total policy. This includes course and curriculum design and course and curriculum organisation, which in turn influence resource implementation. Decisions are made on what to plan (design), how to support the plans (structure) and how to achieve the plans (the organisation), all combining to produce a policy. Implementation of policies and their resource implications are crucial for librarians and for the planning of library resource centres. Policies which relate to resource based learning also interact with other policies, both within the authority and the institution, such as those affecting language, multi-ethnic provision, self-assessment policies, validation and evaluation procedures, and in turn in-service training and staff development policies. Teaching and learning patterns affect independent learning, the role of the teacher as manager, the relationships of departments to other departments and services within the establishment, and in turn, their relationships to the library, all of which have organisational implications. This interdependence of policies, structures and organisational decisions influences the use of resources; all are constantly reinforcing and changing each other, and the library must reflect and support these changes.

This book is not intended to be an up-to-date manual on technical changes and processes, or an academic treatise (both available elsewhere) but a set of frameworks for planning. The aim is to provide a structural basis for resource provision, so that necessary policies and strategies can be worked out in detail, and specific objectives planned within this context of change and interdependence. This general overview, allowing for further detailed planning by individuals, is aimed at school librarians and at those in schools, colleges of further education, sixth form colleges and other centres, who are responsible for the planning, organisation and development of resource centres. Many of the ideas and suggestions may already be familiar, but it is hoped that this structure will bring them together in a coherent way, laying the foundations for action.

This overview also points the way to further information, research and reading, so that each librarian can pursue specific needs in detail as and when required. Works referred to in the text are quoted in the bibliography at the end of each section. Once perspectives and plans have been formulated, particular needs can be updated and changed in relation to local situations. Referring to information sources within broad areas of change and development means that librarians can then obtain current information from a variety of specialist sources, and can personally co-ordinate and utilise this information.

a local 'environment for learning'

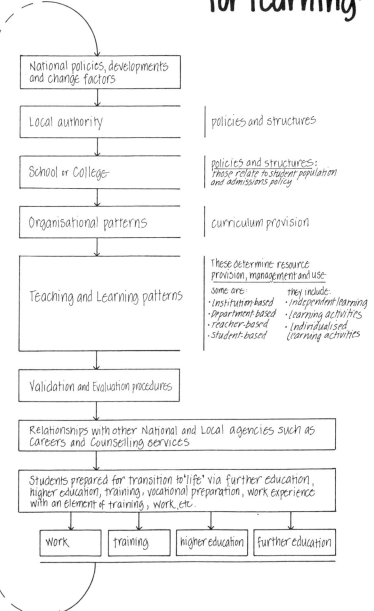

National policies, developments and change factors

Local authority | policies and structures

School or College | policies and structures: those relate to student population and admissions policy

Organisational patterns | curriculum provision

Teaching and Learning patterns |
These determine resource provision, management and use
some are:
· Institution-based
· Department-based
· Teacher-based
· Student-based
they include:
· Independent learning
· learning activities
· Individualised learning activities

Validation and Evaluation procedures

Relationships with other National and Local agencies such as Careers and Counselling services

Students prepared for transition to 'life' via further education, higher education, training, vocational preparation, work experience with an element of training, work, etc.

Work | training | higher education | further education

Part 1
WHY PLAN?
The need to work
within contexts

1   The role of the librarian: planning for change

Recent changes and developments at both national and local levels have affected the role of the library, accelerated the growth of the library resources centre concept, and had an impact on the role of the librarian. The aims and objectives of the library resource centre may well need to be redefined, so that different services can be planned to support these aims and objectives. Hopefully these services will then reflect the changing external forces outlined earlier.

The librarian's role is increasingly both managerial and participative — he or she has a wider range of materials to organise, and a far greater involvement in teaching and learning activities. The role of the librarian and the function of the learning resources centre are inter-linked, as neither can operate in isolation, either from each other, or from the parent establishment. The librarian has to ensure that the resources of the library and the expertise of the staff are fully utilised by and integrated into the whole school curriculum. This includes involvement at the planning, organisational and evaluation stages. The library is central to the learning process or, to quote Bullock, 'the library is at the heart of the school's resources for learning'. If this is to be so, the librarian has to be able to support the work of the school across the total age and ability range, through providing materials, teaching pupils how to use them effectively, and providing support for teachers in their professional areas.

The managerial role

The managerial aspects of the work and the participative and supportive aspects can to some extent be isolated, although again no watertight divisions can be made. The management aspects relate in the main to these areas:

Analysis of the needs of the establishment and of the users;

Policy making — 'contextual' awareness — making sure that the library is not seen as an isolated agent and that policies are integrated into the wider policies of the school/college, and so become part of the structure;

Making decisions on service needs and planning for these needs;

Making decisions on use of space;

Planning the timing and location of such services, including information services etc., and stock evaluation;

Following this, decisions on staffing needs and levels;

Planning *validation* and *evaluation* exercises;

Research.

The participative role

Necessary requirements and activities include:

Involvement in curriculum planning, and in the resultant teaching and learning patterns; making sure that the library responds to these;

Integration with curricular development and organisation, through working with teachers and providing information and new ideas, new materials, and supporting local developments; performing an active educational function; attending relevant meetings in an active role;

Involvement and participation in in-service courses for teachers, including learning skills and information skills;

Making sure that if materials are in the library then the relevant space and equipment is available so that material can be used; work with any technical expertise or support staff to make sure there are no technical gaps in the ways in which materials can be used;

Liaison with staff over the establishment and running of satellite resource centres — these will of course have to reflect subject needs and departmental and/or subject teaching approaches; liaison over stock selection and rejection;

Co-operation over the organisation of displays and exhibitions, in relation to topics which are of national importance, e.g. Children's Book Week, or those which relate to school/college based activities, to help promote the use of the library;

Involvement in any local co-operation inter-lending or networking schemes, or community based activities;

Some understanding of child psychology and child development; some knowledge of reading (processes, levels, development, strategies for teaching, and the fostering of imaginative reading);

Some knowledge and understanding of production activities and the use of media, including the characteristics of information carriers, and the

4

use of media as a stimulus in the teaching and learning situation;

The ability to exploit the traditional skills of librarianship within a curricular context, e.g. bibliographic tools, bibliographic expertise, data processing and information retrieval, research procedures, and literary knowledge to enrich personal growth; all these must relate to materials in all formats;

Involvement in any programme helping students to become effective learners as part of the exploitation of the resources of the library; being involved in any programme helping students to 'learn how to learn';

Co-operation with anyone else in the school or college who can help in exploiting resources, including production staff, design staff, careers and counselling departments.

The supportive role (at technical, clerical and volunteer levels)

It is necessary to make sure that routine tasks, which are unimportant in themselves, but which support any system, are efficient and carried out regularly. If these are not carried out by library staffing (often because support staff is so inadequate) then determine their order of priority and decide when they should be done in the school/college year. It is important to stick to any plan and not to let routines take over from professional managerial or supportive tasks. Routines either computerised or carried out manually, include:

ordering, checking and processing materials, including checking bibliographic references (in all formats);

maintaining a record of finances so that spending can be monitored;

maintaining the shelving system — putting materials in order and re-checking;

maintaining the journal collection;

maintaining a catalogue;

maintaining an issue system, including an overdue system;

checking references in reading lists;

providing photocopies;

circulating periodicals; circulating title pages of journals to support individual subject interests;

ordering items through inter-library loans;

preparing general bibliographies and/or reading lists;

preparing resource lists;

preparing specific/subject bibliographies and/or reading lists;

assisting with users' enquiries;

maintaining files of ephemera relating to current events and particular subject interests (newspaper cuttings etc);

maintaining simple production services;

operating and maintaining routine equipment;

recording off-air broadcasts for schools/colleges.

There has been a lot of controversy in recent years over the qualifications needed by anyone running a library resources centre and carrying out the very demanding role of librarian, and the debate still continues. It would seem that there is no one right answer and that individuals have to make their own decisions in relation to local practice and conditions of service, and individual career patterns.

The majority of librarians working in schools are doing so because that is where they want to be working, but many also feel that they need extra expertise to help them carry out their roles as Heads of Departments. It is possible to qualify as a librarian through a variety of routes, and some courses do include an education component, or lead to dual qualifications in librarianship and education, as advocated by the Bullock report, while others are intended for teachers wishing to qualify as librarians. It would seem from various pieces of research that qualifications in themselves do not necessarily add stature to and acceptance of the role of the school librarian, but in the current climate, the topping up of the initial qualifications as and when needed may provide the most reasonable support. Librarians need to be versatile in areas of educational technology, as well as in educational theory. They would also find courses that relate to linked areas, such as management, counselling and personnel work of value as topping up exercises. As concern for the individual grows, and is reflected in changing courses and provision, librarians need to be able to participate in courses to keep themselves up to date not only in technical areas (such as on-line developments) but also in others that relate to the concern for the student/pupil as a 'whole' person, such as counselling, social patterns and cultural needs. Some of these can be identified within the framework of local and national short courses, some are provided through organisations such as the Open University and the open learning system used by the National Diploma in Educational Technology while others are catered for in the higher educational sphere, through higher research degrees.

initial training: either 3-year courses or 4-year combined course (with education)

or 1-year post graduate certificate

'topping up' in areas such as:

educational technology

management studies

curriculum studies

reading skills

imaginative literature

pastoral care/counselling

multi-ethnic and multi-cultural materials

design and production of materials

information science

higher degrees/research in areas such as:

curriculum studies

information science

comparative studies

specialist areas (e.g. school libraries)

It is also important to be aware of the various and complex numbers of 'routes' through which any trainee or junior members of staff can acquire qualifications at a very basic or intermediate level. These are important, as not only do they contribute to in-service training provision, but increasingly are opening the way for those who would not traditionally enter the profession to do so without formal qualifications, and progress towards degree level courses. To help the profession relate more effectively to its users, the thinking behind the 'traditional' patterns of recruitment currently geared to those who are white, middle class, and frequently female, needs to be changed to increase flexibility in services.

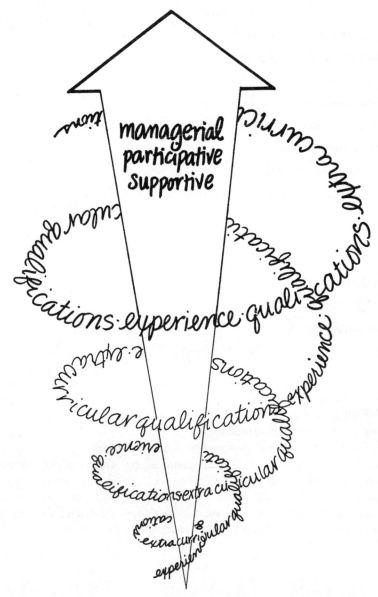

the role of the librarian

● Information — a selective list of relevant groups, institutes and associations

American Association of School
Librarians
50 East Huron Street
Chicago
Illinois 60611
USA

Association for Educational and
Training Technology
BLAT Centre for Health and Medical
Education
BMA House
Tavistock Square
London WC1

ASLIB
3 Belgrave Square
London SW1X 8PL

British Association for Commercial &
Industrial Education (BACIE)
16 Park Crescent
London W1N 4AP

British Association for Counselling
1A Little Church Street
Rugby
Warwick CV21 3AP

British Library, Research and
Development Department
2 Sheraton Street
London W1V 4BH

Industrial Society
Robert Hyde House
48 Bayswater Square
London W1H 1BQ

Institute of Information Scientists
Harvest House
62 London Road
Reading RG1 5AS

Institute of Personnel Management
IPM House
Camp Road
London SW19 4UW

Institute of Training and
Development
5 Baring Road
Beaconsfield
Bucks HP9 2NX

International Federation of Library
Associations (IFLA)
c/o Russell Bowden
Library Association
7 Ridgmount Street
London WC1E 7AE

Library Association
Colleges of Further and Higher
Education Group
Library Association
7 Ridgmount Street
London WC1E 7AE

Library Association
Education Secretary
7 Ridgmount Street
London WC1E 7AE

Library Association
Training and Education Group
Library Association
7 Ridgmount Street
London WC1E 7AE

Library Association
School Libraries Group
Library Association
7 Ridgmount Street
London WC1E 7AE

National Institute for Careers
Education and Counselling
Bayfordbury House
Lower Hatfield Road
Hertford SG13 8LD

Open University
Walton House
Milton Keynes MK7 6AA

School Library Association
Victoria House
29-31 George Street
Oxford OX1 2AY

Society of County Children's
Librarians
c/o Buckinghamshire County Library
Walton Street
Aylesbury
Bucks HP20 1UU

● **Journals — a selective list**

Audiovisual Librarian
Aslib
Library Association Publishing
7 Ridgmount Street
London WC1E 7AE

Current Research
Library Association
7 Ridgmount Street
London WC1E 7AE

Education Libraries Bulletin
University of London Institute of
Education
11-13 Ridgmount Street
London WC1E 7AH

Information and Library Manager
Elm Publications
45 Park Road
Buckden
Cambridgeshire PE18 9SL

Library Management
MCB Publications Ltd
198-200 Keighley Road
Bradford BD9 4JQ

SLG News
School Libraries Group
Library Association
7 Ridgmount Street
London WC1E 7AE

School Librarian
School Library Association
Victoria House
29-31 George Street
Oxford OX1 2XA

School Library Media Quarterly
American Association of School
Librarians
50 East Huron Street
Chicago
Illinois IL60611
USA

Training Officer
20 Cross Street
Manchester M2 1WL

● **References — a selective list of relevant books, reports and articles**

American Association of School Librarians and Association for Educational Communications and Technology. *Media Programmes: District and School.* Chicago, American Library Association and National Education Association, 1975.

Asheim, L. 'Librarians as professionals' in *Library Trends* 27 (3) (Winter 1979), pp 225-57.

Barton, G. 'The Librarian Teacher Course at Froebel Institute College' in *Education Libraries Bulletin 19* (1) Spring 1976, pp 22-8.

Beswick, N. W. 'Double Qualification for Librarians in Schools?' in *Education Libraries Bulletin 21* pt 2 (Summer 1978), pp 40-7.

Beswick, N. W. *Resource Based Learning.* London, Heinemann Educational, 1977.

Beswick, N. W. and Beswick, B. 'Dual Qualification and a career in Educational Librarianship' in *School Librarian 27* (4) December 1979, pp 330-8.

Beswick, N. W. and Beswick, B. 'Teaching and the forward thrust of Librarianship' in *Library Association Record 79* (8) August 1977, p 419.

Campbell, A. 'Training librarians for our schools: recent developments and future possibilities' in *School Librarian 27* (2) June 1979, pp 100-05.

Carroll, F. L. *Recent advances in School Librarianship.* Oxford, Pergamon Press, 1981.

Council for Educational Technology. *Courses leading to qualifications in Educational Technology 1981-1982.* London, Council for Educational Technology, 1981.

Davies, R. A. *The School Library Media Programme: Instructional Force for Excellence.* 3rd ed. London, New York, Bowker, 1979.

Department of Education and Science. *A Language for Life: Report of the Committee of enquiry under the Chairmanship of Sir Alan Bullock.* London, HMSO, 1975. (The Bullock Report).

Directory of Training 1982. Enterprise House, Badgemore Park, Henley-on-Thames, Oxon RG9 4NR.

Education for Librarianship. (tape-slide programme), London, British Council, 1980.

Edwards, H. 'The BA (Hons) Degree course in Education and Library Studies at Loughborough University' in *Education Libraries Bulletin Vol 24* pt. 1 Spring 1981, pp 17-28.

Hamilton, M. 'All things to all men' in *SLA News* (159) September 1980, pp 162-3.

Hannesdottir, S. K.'Education of School Librarians: some alternatives' in *IFLA Journal 6* (1) February 1980, pp 17-24.

Herring, J. E. *School Librarianship.* London, Bingley, 1982.

Libraries and new technology: A Bibliography. London, Library Association,

1980.

Library Association. *College Libraries: recommended standards of library provision in colleges of technology and other establishments of further education.* 2nd rev. ed. London, Library Association, 1971.

Library Association. *Directory of short courses in Librarianship and information work.* London, Library Association.

Library Association. *Libraries and resource centres: A statement. LAR 76* (12) December 1974.

Library Association. *Library resource provision in schools: Guidelines and Recommendations.* London, Library Association, 1977.

Library Association. *Recommended salary grades and conditions of service for School Librarians.* London, Library Association, 1982.

Library Association. *Report of the working party on training.* London, Library Association, 1977.

Library Association. *School library resource centres: Recommended standards for policy and provision.* London, Library Association, 1970.

Library Association. *School library resource centres: Recommended standards for policy and provision, a supplement on non book materials.* London, Library Association, 1972.

Library Association. *Working party on the future of professional qualifications: Recommendations of the implementation board.* London, Library Association, 1977.

Library Association. *Working party on the future of professional qualifications: Recommendations of the implementation board.* London, Library Association, 1978.

Library Association, Colleges of Further and Higher Education Group. *College Libraries and guidelines for professional service and resource provision.* 3rd rev. ed. London, Library Association, 1978.

Marland, M. 'Tough on Assignments' in *Times Educational Supplement,* 18 July 1980 p.18.

National Association of Teachers in Further and Higher Education. *College Libraries: Policy Statement.* London, NATFHE, 1982.

National Association of Teachers in Further and Higher Education. *Student Counselling.* London, NATFHE, 1979.

School Libraries in Britain. (tape slide programme), London, British Council, 1980.

School Library Association. *The staffing of secondary school libraries.* Oxford, School Library Association, 1970.

School Library Association. *The Way Ahead.* Oxford, School Library Association, 1980.

Shaffer, D. E. *Criteria for improving the professional status of Librarianship.* Arlington, Educational Resources Information Centre, 1980.

Shrigley, R. M. 'The rocky road' in *New Library World 78* (929) November 1977, pp 206-7.

Ward, N. (ed.) *Which Library School?* 2nd ed., London, AAL, 1982.

Wood, K. *Professional Qualifications: What will happen in 1981? Library Association Record 81* (12) December, 1979, pp 577, 579, 581.

Wylie, T. *Counselling young people.* Leicester, National Youth Bureau, 1980.

Planning pointers

- Analyse your needs in relation to your specific work situation and to your long term career ambitions.

- Relate changing demands of the curriculum to personal development.

- See how many demands and needs both current and potential can be satisfied through local or national provision. Is this feasible and practical in relation to time, length of courses, staffing problems and fees?

- What alternative methods could be used? Are there locally available courses which could be cannibalised for a group of librarians? Are there teachers taking evening classes which could be helpful? Is any of the open learning provision relevant?

- If necessary form a local user/pressure group. It is very possible that a large institution in the area (university or polytechnic) can be persuaded to run cost effective 'tailor made' courses if they are aware of demand.

- Keep up to date with courses designed for 'alternative methods of entry into and training within the profession'.

2   Change factors: background to planning

Changes in curriculum planning and organisation are slow, and occur at a variety of levels and for many reasons. Some main strands can be isolated, although there are many factors and events that contribute to the total picture. Changes must be seen as part of the national and international flow of ideas. Nothing stands in isolation and certainly not in the educational sphere, using 'education' in its broadest possible sense. No librarian can possibly be au fait with all developments, but it is important to maintain an interest in what is happening, and why, so that planning and provision is not a last minute hurried retreat into action, but an integrated, long term and constantly adapting operation.

Change is slow, partly because so many forces are involved, but a survey of some major influences will illustrate the organisations and national bodies that exert pressure. These forces tend to cluster together under the umbrellas of educational changes, social and economic factors, industrial factors, and an interlinking thread of political movements.

Within this atmosphere of concern and alteration, there are also other change elements, including the lack of further educational and training opportunities for the vast majority of school leavers, the current piecemeal provision, a decline in the post school population, and of course, political change and uncertainty. Examinations and the examination system also inevitably block change, in addition to causing it, and the effects of examinations around the age of 16 tend to put a brake on any innovation that started in the primary sector and the first years of secondary education. This 'dulling' effect is also echoed by the universities, where the wider approaches aimed for at the secondary level tend to become slowly altered to compartmentalised subject specialisms (as vividly illustrated in the 'structuralist' row at Cambridge in 1981).

Teaching and learning

One of the most important elements in the whole shifting picture has been that of changes in the patterns of teaching and learning, and this element is the one that has probably had the greatest effect on library resource centres. These changes cover a wide spectrum, from the introduction of programmed learning machines, to computer assisted learning. There is a considerable literature on this subject, and some of the major works are listed in the bibliography. Beswick's *Resource Based Learning* covers many aspects, and it is fruitless to reproduce here detailed synopses of the works of Gagne and Bloom for example.

Those changes have included, among others, the hardware revolution, the integrated day in the primary sector, the re-thinking of the use of spaces, the development of satellite resource centres, and the involvement of a variety of curriculum teams at local and institutional levels. All these have in turn been part of the changing pattern of provision, including comprehensivisation (partly responsible for the increase in mixed ability teaching), changes in further education provision, with an increasing concern for the less academic pupils, and alterations in organisational patterns at sixth form level. The need to prepare pupils for the world of work in relation to their individual capabilities, as well as in practical preparation through the acquisition of communication skills, physical skills and basic literacy and numeracy, has also added impetus to changing patterns. All have helped show the need to provide learning materials for a wide range of students. Existing 'standard' texts and traditional methods of teaching were not compatible with new trends, and so alternatives were designed and produced. The provision of such materials, for resource assisted teaching, for resource based teaching and, more slowly, for resource based learning, as well as individualised learning for students, were produced both at the national, local and 'in-house' levels, leading to enormous problems of production, storage and retrieval. It was the latter tasks of storage and retrieval that drew most librarians into the resources arena, rather than those of curriculum design and the production of materials, and the situation remains largely unchanged.

Much of the literature is concerned with the organisation of resources material, and little else. However the picture is no longer static, as libraries and librarians are increasingly involved in course planning, course production and the effective exploitation of materials, rather than being passive organisers of documents. This development is a consequence of the introduction of radical, although often exam orientated curricular changes, including the work of the re-named Business and Technician Education Council, who may merge to form a more powerful national body, the advent of computer assisted and computer managed learning, the use of Prestel and the development of sophisticated data bases. The emphasis by the Business and Technician Education Council on individual work, tailored to local needs, and leaning heavily on the use of resource materials, and thence on the use of libraries, has added to the impetus. Prior to their merger both these Councils have also contributed to changes in curriculum methodology through their introduction of educational technology concepts in planning. Many materials for the new courses are 'in-house' but cut across existing boundaries (cross-modular assignments) and need support by libraries for both teacher and student. City and Guilds Foundation courses and the Royal Society of Arts course have also added impetus, in their resource based courses for the lower levels of vocational work. The open access philosophy of many Further Education Colleges has also contributed to the growth of pre-vocational and vocational (technical) courses, as new entrants to colleges increasingly belong to a group who are unable to find jobs, unsure of what they want to do, and lack advice. The development of individual 'learning agendas' has also been an area of development in this field, and will doubtless affect thinking in the school sector. All the changes in and decrease in the number of apprenticeship schemes have also had an effect. The latest Government initiatives have however offset some of the effects of the decline in these opportunities, and have added a 'skill' dimension to the previous 'time' dimension. All courses concerned with skills are aiming at making the acquisition of such skills as flexible as possible, and as wide ranging as possible.

Other changes in this area have affected libraries and their role, and are still doing so. On one hand there is current concern with the acquisition of the so-called 'life and social skills', autonomous learning, provision for a multi-cultural society (including the establishment of the Educational Disadvantage Unit), and the closing of social gaps, and on the other the thinking towards more central control, a core curriculum, and the comparatively recent establishment of the Assessment of Performance Unit.

The Department of Education and Science

The DES, with its national responsibilities and working in conjunction with local and regional administrations, has also contributed to curricular change, both through its published reports and advisory documents, issued centrally, and through the work and publications of the Further Education Curriculum Review and Development Unit, which now has company status and a simplified title: 'Further Education Unit'. During the past few years these reports and papers have become increasingly part of the total national concern with the need to prepare pupils and students for the transition from school and college to work. These reports should be seen by librarians as clearly relating to major publications issued by other related organisations, such as the Manpower Services Commission and the Confederation of British Industry. Many current ideas echo those of earlier reports, and the pattern clearly emerging is of relevant flexible provision, responding to national and local needs. Access courses, bridging courses, school-college links, 'New Opportunities' courses and 'Second Chance' courses are all examples of these changes. The concern with the move towards a core curriculum, as illustrated in many of the recent DES publications, also has implications for a nationally implemented policy.

Earlier official reports, such as Newsom and Crowther, were concerned with the relevance and practicability of curricula offered in schools, and later reports have both echoed this concern, reflected current thinking on a core curriculum and been concerned with the current problems of the 'under achievers'. Such curricular changes must inevitably influence library provision and use, and emphasise the need for librarians to relate and adapt to change. The key reports should be familiar to all those who are in the education field and acting as potential agents for change. Many current ideas are not new but echo the concepts of Crowther, such as the need for communication skills (literacy, oracy and numeracy), knowledge and understanding of the physical and social environment, moral and aesthetic sensibilities and, finally, the need to be able to express personal ideas (the creative and expressive arts). Newsom too was concerned with ideas that are at present under discussion, such as the acquisition of basic skills, and the need to provide work experience, as well as the re-inforcement of basic skills through every medium of the curriculum. None of these ideas can be divorced from social and economic pressures, which in turn are reflected by the work and publications of bodies such as the Manpower Services Commission, the Department of Employment, the Confederation of British Industry, the National Association of Teachers in Further and Higher Education, the Council for Educational Technology, and the Industrial Society — all of these provide pointers for librarians, and guides to planning.

The White Paper of 1972 was concerned with implementing Rosla and with expansion in the secondary sector. It was also concerned with the Diploma in Higher Education, a foundation course for further study, and a radical departure in that it offered a viable alternative to existing courses of study, and to increased mobility for students, with implications for the provision, availability and use of resources. The report in 1976 on *Curricula for non-participant 16-19's* also reflected current changes, and again has resource implications, as has *Educational Disadvantage: perspectives and policies*, with implications relating to disadvantaged sectors and communities, and particularly to the whole problem of providing for a multi-cultural society. The latter also links with the work of the now established Educational Disadvantage Unit. *Curriculum 11–16* (1977) reflected the views of the Inspectorate on core areas of experience. The concern for the needs of the multi-cultural classroom now also includes the broader area of concern for the Third World, with curricular and resource implications. *Unified Vocational Preparation: a pilot approach* is also important, partly as it led to the establishment of the Further Education Curriculum Review and Development Unit, with its policy of providing a centre for curriculum review, dissemination and development at a national level, and partly because it was a joint publication with the Department of Industry, illustrating an increasingly close liaison between the two departments. The Unified Vocational Preparation scheme has integrated education and training, and also includes personal and vocational elements, aimed particularly at young people entering work. The publications of the Further Education Unit, as indicated later, are crucial, as they are all relevant to the changing curriculum, and to increasingly flexible learning opportunities.

Other DES initiatives are reflected in publications such as *Local Authority arrangements for the school curriculum*, published in 1979, which tried to establish a national consensus for establishing a framework for the curriculum by surveying existing arrangements, and preliminary ideas on this were presented in *A Framework for the school curriculum*, issued in 1980. This latter document was intended to act as a basis for guidance and discussion to local authorities. In both reports there are attempts to set suggestions within a social context, and also implications for resource provision at national, local and institutional levels, in relation to 'core' areas established, multi-cultural materials, patterns at sixth form level, and the relationships between schools, further education and work. The survey of 1979 mentioned above reflected the inspectors' finding on the curriculum and included the statement that 'the school library is the most important single contribution of all to the school's reading resources' (pp. 79-81). The interesting aspect of this was that they were not optimistic about the effectiveness of policies as a result of the Bullock Report and thereby the effect, or lack of it, on school libraries and librarians. (Their opinions are supported by the recent damning survey by the DES of 10 per cent of the country's school libraries.) What has now emerged as a potential core curriculum covers English and Mathematics, the Humanities, Science, plus Design and Technology — it is easy to identify the roots behind these labels.

The need to equip pupils to cope with society and for schools to be aware of wider issues than 'traditional' exam subjects is again reflected in the recommendations issued in 1981 *(The School Curriculum)* and the similar Schools Council report of the same year *(The Practical Curriculum)*. Students in the post-compulsory age group are the subject of several papers issued in 1979 *(Providing educational opportunities for 16-18 year olds, A better start in working life* issued with the Department of Employment and Industry, and *16-18: Education and Training for 16-18 year olds: a consultative paper*, also issued with the Department of Employment). All are concerned with the patterns and organisation of educational provision, including sixth form and tertiary colleges, and with the deployment of resources — both crucial to the library profession. The Macfarlane Report of 1981 has also contributed to the debate. The issue is still very much under consideration, and unless library provision is built into these changes, it will be impossible to make up for lost time later.

The same increasingly unified approach, i.e. not isolated from external pressures, is clearly illustrated by the Further Education Unit reports. Major reports are listed in the bibliography, and are concerned with the broadening of curriculum content, plus related teaching and learning patterns for the post sixteen age group. The work of the unit has also affected the organisation of courses — some are now based in colleges, some in industry, some link local educational provision and industry, but all are innovative, concerned with change, and mirror the need for and provision of different and far less 'watertight' courses. Both the content and the process of curricular innovation and broadening is important for these students, and teachers need to be increasingly concerned with the learning needs of the students, rather than teaching methods. The unit has not only surveyed existing provision (*Signposts*, 1981), but has also issued guidance for tutors involved in this work (*Developing Social and Life Skills* 1980), and suggestions for college support (*Supporting YOP* 1979, and *A Basis for Choice* 1979). The resourcing of these courses must be equally flexible, and demands close integration between the planners of the courses, those who teach them, and the providers and organisers of resources (the librarians) and student involvement.

Students participating in many of these courses may well be disadvantaged (socially, educationally, or physically) or may have opted out from the authoritarian regime of school, and so there is a need for librarians to establish sympathetic and understanding attitudes towards this 'new constituency'. The same applies to those taking newer courses, such as the City and Guilds courses based in school. Librarians must ensure that not only are they themselves aware of these developments, but the planning and therefore the system and the stock supports these students. Help is available, both through reading the publications, liaising with 'experts' within the institution, and having available any materials quoted. As these departments and bodies begin to work together at both state and local level, so must librarians relax their boundaries, and be perceptive of change and innovation, and prepare themselves for it. The increasing involvement of libraries with community groups is another example of the blurring of the boundaries at local levels, and of an increasing sensitivity to change. The economic situation has helped in the consideration of the use of buildings and plant, and in some ways has added impetus to the ideas of community services and community schools, linked to or part of library services. To support and train personnel for such changes there is an abundance of courses up and down the country which are helpful and relevant, not all necessarily labelled 'for librarians', and they form yet another supportive strand in the changing situation.

The Manpower Services Commission

The work of the Manpower Services Commission is another strand in this web, and its most important work, the Holland Report (*Young people and work* 1977) attempted to provide, through the Youth Opportunities Programme, coherent provision of opportunities, particularly for the young unemployed, within a framework of the needs and demands of society and industry. The majority of courses contain an element of further education thus giving the education world an important role in the programme, and involving curriculum design and implementation, so that again library resources and facilities are part of the picture. Current provision on the Youth Opportunities Programme may include day release in colleges to acquire relevant qualifications, with resultant services implications for libraries and the assessment of both the inter-face and tightly regularised (and inflexible!) procedures. The report in itself is an example of change resulting from pressures, and of the increasing blurring of boundaries as a response to these pressures, as it included reports from, among others, the Confederation of British Industry, the DES, and the Trades Union Congress, all of whom are aware of the need to respond to change in the education and training process. The training initiative announced in December 1981 and operational as from 1983, includes a billion pound package called the 'Youth Training Scheme' intended to replace the YOP scheme, and to provide a comprehensive and state-funded training package for all those leaving school and unable to get a job, and providing work experience, education and training. These initiatives, called the 'New Training Initiatives' have involved consultation with industry as well as educationalists, again illustrating the extent of this problem, and showing how it cannot be compartmentalised into one neat area. Other MSC reports have been concerned with the whole area of vocational preparation, with setting up skill teaching schemes in schools, and with the acquisition of 'life' skills which, despite the title, includes a strong element of information, i.e. learning skills. All are concerned with widening the narrow concept of skills and providing relevant and broader learning opportunities. The challenge to both education and other agencies is to equip students with skills to cope with work and with changes in their personal lives, and this means the re-thinking of many traditional approaches — new alternatives are needed. Students and pupils are already moving into the area of a negotiated curriculum, which brings the problem of assessment into the limelight. This again illustrates the thread, from Crowther and Newsom, through the work of the MSC, to the current preoccupation of librarians with user education and, hopefully, learning skills. This concern with the need to learn how to learn is the core of the recent Schools Council (1982) publication on information skills. The MSC continues its work in the training and vocational field, by producing surveys of need, and through proposing the establishment of the 'Open Tech', to provide training and retraining for adults at technician level, and now moving into basic management training, using distance learning techniques. This proposal fits in with yet another impetus, the provision of recurrent and continuing educational opportunities. The challenge of innovation in this area cannot be met until teachers and librarians have adjusted and responded to change and have come to terms with a re-allocation of resources, and with the necessary changes in organisation to ensure this.

An increasing awareness of the need for recurrent and continuing educational opportunities, continuing from the Russell Report, and provided in part through open learning systems, will also involve librarians in this area. Open learning has been defined as a system which enables individuals to participate in programmes of study regardless of where they live, and of their circumstances, and which allows them to study on their own and at a pace convenient to them as individuals, so that they are involved in their own choice of aims and objectives. It thus centres on their needs as individuals, is problem centred, and combines many methods, resources, and arrangements to provide this situation. These changes will also ensure that librarians are increasingly involved in managerial decisions on the availability and provision of library services for those involved in open learning, and so there will have to be some re-thinking of the 'traditional' approaches, including attitudes to basic services, opening hours, other services offered, and relationships with agencies such as counselling and referral agencies. The concept revolves around the idea of access, and the individual tailoring of courses to individual student needs will also necessarily involve librarians in course planning and development, as well as in the provision of resources, and in answering questions revolving around the actual need for materials, such as: Who will use these materials? What will they need? Who will produce them? How and where will they be organised? Although many of these changes are at present under the aegis of 'adult education', the boundaries are becoming increasingly blurred.

The examination structure

Another aspect of the changes that occur in the curriculum as a result of administrative changes includes examination structures, which in turn are part of national developments. For example, the Haslegrave Committee had as part of its brief the rationalisation of existing technician courses. However it also developed a new range of courses which are college based, and depend heavily on resource materials for projects in subject areas and in most modular (inter-disciplinary) assignments. The same dependence on resource use applies to the Business Education Council courses, also established to rationalise existing provision. The Technician Education Council and the Business Education Council have now merged and form one common body — the Business and Technician Education Council. Other curricular changes, within the constraints illustrated, have also stemmed from the work of the Schools Council, which in its new and more vigorous post 1978 format, has as one of its major responsibilities that of developing the curriculum in relation to changing needs. This is clearly stating what has been an area of concern for the Council for many years, and its documents have long been pertinent to the work of librarians (or if they haven't, should have been). *General studies 16-18* was concerned with change, as was *Cross'd with adversity*, which was concerned with socially disadvantaged pupils. The involvement of the Council in the post-school years is illustrated in working paper 33, produced in 1971. Many other publications have inevitably been examination based, dated from working paper 5 in 1965, to working papers 45 and 46 in 1971. Proposals for the now defunct CEE were made in 1975, and for a common system of examination at 16+ in 1971. The valuable Schools Council Curriculum projects (such as the General Studies Project) also had an impact on resource materials and their use and organisation, both in the classroom and in libraries. Joint projects involving the Nuffield Foundation were also important, as was the Nuffield Resources for Learning Project, established as a result of the proliferation of resource materials from the Nuffield Foundation Projects. All have contributed to the resource centre 'movement' and its effect on library practices.

Both the DES and the Schools Council are also heavily involved in controversial proposals for a new examination system at 16+, and are stressing that it must be possible to change suggestions so that the curriculum does not become static. Syllabuses, methodology and assessment will also change, including an increasing amount of assessed course work and multi-disciplinary or general studies work. Current proposals (1982) to establish separate bodies to deal with examinations and curriculum change will, regardless of their format, have resource implications, as have the proposals for a pre-vocational examination at 17+ (Certificate of Pre-Vocational Education), aimed particularly at the group regarded as the 'new sixth form', whose needs have tended to be neglected.

The City and Guilds courses and examinations, as well as those of the Royal Society of Arts, have also had implications for course planning and resource provision as both include project work. City and Guilds responds to changing demands by offering to produce both new courses and examinations when requested by colleges. The RSA is in the process of changing its syllabus to include an increasing emphasis on modern technology, including information science, and is responding to the need to re-assess education and training for the business world. As many of its course are school and college based and contain a 'library element' these will need support in the form of resource materials and increased co-operation over teaching input. Flexibility is needed by librarians in adapting to other new courses, such as changing A levels, 'Access' and 'New Opportunity' courses, those offered by the National Extension College and through the Training Opportunities Programme of the MSC. Many of these are not necessarily taught in the classroom, and can be based on distance learning principles, or be prepared as individual study modules, located in the library. The same need for flexibility and imagination applies to the resourcing of the courses initiated by the remaining Industrial Training Boards, many of which contain a strong further education element.

Industrial factors

Another area concerns industrial influence and this has been strong, as industrial needs, in terms of manpower planning and provision, are part of the economic and social picture, and bodies such as the Industrial Society and the Confederation of British Industry are closely involved in the development between educational planning and industry. Curricular changes follow alterations in courses both at the advanced level, and at the school — college, school — industry links level. Resources need to support those involved in the teaching and learning of such courses (including A levels in industrial studies) but there is a clear distinction between information and resource materials concerning industry, and programmes and courses for those being educated and trained for a specific area. There is a need for education and industry to move much more closely together, and for a more realistic information network to be set up. The remaining Industrial Training Boards have a role to play as many of their courses are partly located in further education establishments, and courses have to be planned in relation to training needs and to patterns of student release, so that again library services will be affected. Course aims and objectives will have to be matched to employment needs, so that teacher training and re-training is also affected, increasingly offering the chance for librarians to have an 'input' in initial teacher training courses. Schools too need to keep pupils more closely informed of industrial activities, and need information on careers and locally based work experience schemes, hence the need for the information network. Schools also base courses geared to local industries within a local 'linking' framework, with implications for resourcing the curriculum, in the design and the supply of materials. The social implications of preparing young people for the world of work, and ensuring that they have the necessary 'survival skills' are also important, and the transition period of school to work, and university to industry, is the thread that links many of these problems. They are recognised by organisations such as the Grubb Institute and its Industrial Tutors.

The library must respond to national and local needs, and so must be aware of national and local initiatives, and many of these are springing up in inner city areas. Packs may be produced, as there is little material available commercially, and in the planning of a CSE project, for example, library expertise could and should be added to the planning of a course. Some materials may already be part of library stocks, and effective exploitation must be based on a detailed knowledge of materials. There may well also be scope for local co-operative initiatives in the housing and indexing of materials.

The media

The media also affect libraries, including the production and use of materials for curriculum support, curriculum extension, in-service training, up-to-date information, and also in extending the role of libraries and librarians. This includes their participation in the Adult Literacy Campaign and in programmes such as the *Road Show*. The latter was concerned with publicising information sources on social and legal rights to the post-sixteen age group. The Gulbenkian Foundation's recent study on *Broadcasting and Youth* was concerned with this problem, and recommended more relevant programmes for young people. There is an increasing potential for co-operation between the media, those involved in work with young people, and bodies such as Youthaid and the National Youth Bureau. This extension of role may not fall into such a neat administrative area, such as Schools Broadcasting, but has enormous potential including an active information, publicity, and community role for libraries. The whole world of Channel Four and its educational potential has yet to be determined, but will undoubtedly have an effect on both co-operation and the use of resources, so that both libraries and the planners and producers of media can interact in a much more informed and positive way. Hopefully the services involved in the broadcasting, educational, and librarianship worlds will begin to interact in context, as many of their core aims are shared, particularly those of education and the uses of information. There is also ample scope for libraries to provide a wider range of more imaginative materials to support programmes devised for school and college students. It goes without saying that notes and programme notes should be in the school library, but information on courses and counselling services which support educational and personal counselling programmes can also form part of the library support for such programmes. The library can act as a focal point for information on programmes, and then help support teachers through alerting them to relevant resources and acting as a stimulus in lesson planning. Some programmes, such as those dealing with continuing education, can also lead to a more informed and united use of resources, involving local history collections, archives, museum collections and specialist personnel — many of which are frequently under-exploited or exploited in isolation. Some programmes can also be used by librarians as support when they are involved in teacher induction activities. There is also scope for many supportive and follow-up activities, with their roots in community activities.

Counselling and community services offered up and down the country through radio, TV and local action groups, should link with existing information services in libraries, and should provide impetus for improving and extending these. This potential for furthering a collaborative and effective use of library resources is also considered later in more detail. Not only have the media formed part of this network of change, but they too have caused the profession to look at its existing services and ideas, and begin to re-assess the service needs, and to consider the training and re-training needs of its own personnel.

The new technology

The increasing use of the media is one facet of increasingly fast technological changes. These include among other developments the processing, storage, retrieval and dissemination and use of information, and particularly of current and fast changing information, such as on-line information, increasingly specialised data bases, the use of word processors, electronic mail, electronic data publishing, increasingly sophisticated links between video and computers, and local area networks. Videotex and Prestel have a place to play in all this and, even at the current innovative stage, have contributed to education change and an awareness of the potential of viewdata in many contexts, particularly those of information skills. The development of telesoftware is also crucial, as this offers a national base for the distribution of computer programmes, thus increasing their availability, and making radical changes in teaching and learning patterns. The newly established Microelectronics Education Programme represents a national plan, which is intended to prepare pupils for a society in which the new technology forms an integral part. The programme aims to develop the curriculum and provides teacher training and re-training facilities and the necessary support for resource provision and organisation. All three areas of change relate to library provision and practice, and to improved in-service training and management techniques in the application and use of the new technology. The programme is based at Newcastle, but also includes national co-ordinators and regional information and training centres.

All these changes in the educational sphere have had effects on the role and status of the librarian, and on the stock of the library resource centre, widening it from the narrower concepts of print based materials to those produced in the form of tapes, slides, packages, videos, films, video discs, compact discs, VICs, computer programmes, and a host of others. The whole area of new technology has had, and will have, increasing implications for the acquisition of new skills, for changes in attitude, and for facilitating new teaching and learning methods. These in turn will have implications far beyond the boundaries of librarianship.

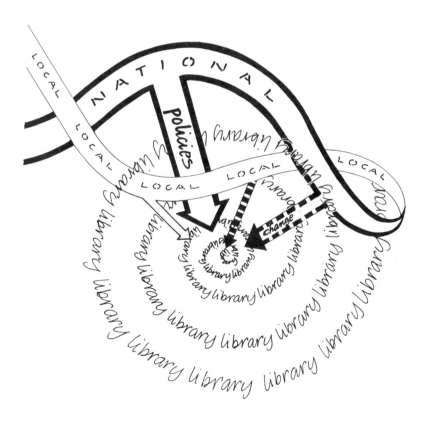

Adult Literacy and Basic Skills Unit
52/4 High Holborn
London WC1

Advisory Centre for Education (ACE)
18 Victoria Park Square
London E2

Advisory Council for Adult and
Continuing Education (ACACE)
19b De Montfort Street
Leicester LE1 7GE

Association for Recurrent Education
(ARE)
Secretary: Arthur Gould
Loughborough University
Loughborough
Leics LE11 3TU

Association of Colleges of Further
and Higher Education (ACFHE)
Secretary: ACFHE
Sheffield City Polytechnic
Sheffield S1 1WB

British Association for Counselling
1a Little Church Street
Rugby CV21 3AP

British Broadcasting Corporation
(BBC)
Educational Liaison Officers
The Langham
London W1A 1AA

British Computer Society
13 Mansfield Street
London W1

British Educational Administration
Society
Moray House College
Holyrood Road
Edinburgh EH8 8AQ

British Library
Research and Development
Department
2 Sheraton Street
London W1V 4BH

British Library Information Officer for
User Education
Loughborough University of
Technology
Loughborough
Leics LE11 3TU

Business Education Council (BEC)
Berkshire House
High Holborn
London WC1V 7AG

Careers and Occupational
Information Centre (COIC)
The Pennine Centre
20-22 Hawley Street
Sheffield S1 3GA

Careers Research and Information
Service
Bateman Street
Cambridge CB2 1LZ

Centre for Continuing Education
The Open University
PO Box 188
Milton Keynes MK3 6HW

Centre for Extension Studies
University of Loughborough
Loughborough
Leics LE11 3TU

Centre for Research on User Studies
(CRUS)
University of Sheffield
Western Bank
Sheffield S10 2TN

Channel 4
60 Charlotte Street
London W1

Chartered Institute of Public Finance
and Accountancy (CIPFA)
1 Buckingham Place
London SW1E 6HS

City and Guilds of London Institute
(CGLI)
76 Portland Place
London W1N 4AA

CLRS Reference Library and
Information Service
ILEA Centre for Learning Resources
275 Kennington Lane
London SE11 5QZ

Commission for Racial Equality
(CRE)
Elliot House
10/12 Allington Street
London SW1E 5EH

Community Education Development
Centre
c/o Stoke School
Briton Road
Coventry CV2 4LF

Confederation of British Industry
(CBI)
Centre Point
New Oxford Street
London WC1

Council for Educational Technology
(CET)
3 Devonshire Street
London W1N 2BA

Department of Education and
Science (DES)
Assessment of Performance Unit
Elizabeth House
York Road
London SE1 7PH

Department of Industry
Industry Education Unit
Ashdown House
123 Victoria Street
London SW1

Education Management Information
Exchange
National Foundation for Educational
Research
The Mere
Upton Park
Slough
Berks SL1 2DQ

Educational Television Association
86 Micklegate
York
YO1 1JZ

European Association of Teachers
20 Brookfield
Highgate West Hill
London N6 6AS

Federation of Open Learning Colleges
Barnet College
Wood Street
Barnet
Herts

Further Education Unit
Department of Education and
Science
Elizabeth House
York Road
London SE1 7PH

Further Education Research Network
FERN Co-ordinators
Centre for Postgraduate Studies in
Education and Research
Leicester Polytechnic
Leicester LE7 9SU

Further Education Staff College
Coombe Lodge
Blagdon
Bristol BS18 6RG

General Studies Association
75 Park Road
Sutton Coldfield
B73 6BO

Grubb Institute of Behavioural
Studies
The EWR Centre
Cloudesley Street
London N1

Gulbenkian Foundation
98 Portland Place
London W1N 4ET

Industrial Language Research Unit
Ltd
32 Trumpington Street
Cambridge

Industrial Society
Robert Hyde House
48 Bryanston Square
London W1H 1BQ

International Broadcasting Trust
9 Upper Berkeley Street
London W1H 8BY

International Federation of Library
Associations (IFLA)
c/o Russell Bowden
Library Association
7 Ridgmount Street
London WC1E 7AE

Library Advisory Council for England
c/o Office of Arts and Libraries
Elizabeth House
York Road
London SE1 7PH

Local Government Training Board
Arndale House
Arndale Centre
Luton LU1 2TS

Manpower Services Commission
(MSC)
Selkirk House
166 High Holborn
London WC1V 6PF

Microelectronics Education Project
(MEP)
Director: R. Fothergill
Cheviot House
Coach Lane Campus
Newcastle upon Tyne NE7 7XA

National Association for Careers
Education and Counselling
Bayfordsbury House
Lower Hatfield Road
Hertford

National Association for Multiracial
Education (NAME)
48 Lewisham High Street
London SE13

National Association for Remedial
Education
2 Litchfield Road
Stafford
Staffs ST17 4JX

National Association for Staff
Development in Further and Higher
Education
Redgrave House
Prestbury
Macclesfield
Cheshire SK10 4BW

National Association of Teachers in
Further and Higher Education
(NATFHE)
Hamilton House
Mabledon Place
London WC1H 9BH

National Centre for Industrial
Language Training
The Havelock Centre
Havelock Road
Southall
Middlesex

National Centre for School
Technology
Trent Polytechnic
Burton Street
Nottingham NG1 4RU

National Conference of Teachers'
Centre Leaders
c/o Hipper Teachers' Centre
Markham Road
Chesterfield
Derbyshire

National Council for Voluntary
Organisations
26 Bedford Square
London WC1B 3HU

National Extension College (NEC)
8 Brooklands Avenue
Cambridge CB2 2HN

National Foundation for
Educational Research (NFER)
including the
Education Management
Information Exchange
Educational Policy
Information Division
Local Research
Consultancy Service
The Mere
Upton Park
Slough
Berks SL1 2DQ

National Institute of Careers
Education and Counselling
Bayfordbury House
Lower Hatfield Road
Hertford SG13 8LQ

National Reprographic Centre for
Documentation
Hatfield Polytechnic
Bayfordbury
Hertford SG13 8LD

National Union of Teachers (NUT)
Hamilton House
Mabledon Place
London WC1H 9BH

National Youth Bureau
17/23 Albion Street
Leicester

Nuffield Foundation
Nuffield Lodge
Regent's Park
London NW1 4RS

Open Learning Federation
Nye Rowlands
Fielden Park College
Barlow Moor Road
West Didsbury
Manchester M20 8PQ

Open University
Milton Keynes
MK7 6AA

Oxfam
Oxfam Education Department
(Third World Studies)
274 Banbury Road
Oxford

Resources for Learning Unit
Redcross Street
Bristol BS2 0BA

Royal Society of Arts (RSA)
18 John Adam Street
London WC2N 6AJ

School Broadcasting Council for the
United Kingdom
The Langham
Portland Place
London W1A 1AA

School Library Association
Victoria House
29-31 George Street
Oxford OX1 2AY

Schools Council
160 Great Portland Street
London W1N 6LL

Schools Council Industry Project
29 Maiden Lane
Covent Garden
London WC2

Scottish Adult Basic Education Unit
Broadcasting Resource Bank
Network Premises
Dowanhill
The Victoria Crescent Road
Glasgow G12 9JN

Scottish Business Education Council
22 Great King Street
Edinburgh EH3 6QH

Scottish Centre for Educational
Technology
12 Rose Street
Glasgow G3

Scottish Technical Education Council
38 Queen Street
Glasgow G1 3DY

Society for Academic Gaming and
Simulation
Centre for Extension Studies
Loughborough University of
Technology
Loughborough
Leics LE11 3TU

Society for Research into Higher
Education Ltd
University of Surrey
Guildford
Surrey GU2 5XH

Society of County Children's
Librarians
c/o Buckinghamshire County Library
Walton Street
Aylesbury
Bucks HP20 1UU

Technician Education Council (TEC)
Central House
Upper Woburn Place
London WC1H 0HH

Trident Trust
11 York Terrace East
Regents Park
London NW1 4PT

Understanding British Industry
21 Tothill Street
London SW1 9LP

Work Research Unit
Steel House
11 Tothill Street
London SW1H 9NF

Workers Educational Association
(WEA)
9 Upper Berkeley Street
London W1H 8BY

Young Volunteer Force Foundation
7 Leonard Street
London EC2A 4AQ

Youthaid
Tress House
3 Stamford Street
London SE1 9NT

● **Journals — a selective list**

ARE Newsletter
Secretary of Association for
Recurrent Education: Arthur Gould
Loughborough University
Loughborough
Leics LE11 3TU

Aslib Proceedings
Aslib
3 Belgrave Square
London SW1X 8PL

BEC News
Business Education Council
Berkshire House
High Holborn
London WC1V 7AG

British Education Index (BEI)
Library Association
7 Ridgmount Street
London WC1E 7AE

British Educational Research Journal
British Educational Research
Association
Carfax Publishing Company
PO Box 25
Abingdon
Oxfordshire OX14 1RW

British Humanities Index (BHI)
Library Association
7 Ridgmount Street
London WC1E 7AE

*British Journal of Educational
Technology*
Council for Educational Technology
3 Devonshire Street
London W1N 2BA

British Library News
British Library
2 Sheraton Street
London W1V 4BH

CBI Education and Training Bulletin
Confederation of British Industry
Centre Point
New Oxford Street
London WC1

CES Review
Centre for Environmental Studies
62 Chandos Place
London WC2N 4HH

Community Education Network
Community Education Development
Centre
Briton Row
Coventry CV2 4LF

Computers and Education
Pergamon Press
Headington Hill Hall
Oxford OX3 0BW

Coombe Lodge Reports
Further Education Staff College
Coombe Lodge
Blagdon
Bristol BS18 6RG

Department of Education and
Science Statistical Bulletin
Elizabeth House
York Road
London SE1

Educa
Guildford Educational Services Ltd
164 High Street
Guildford
Surrey

Education
Longmans
Fourth Avenue
Harlow
Essex

Education Journal
Commission for Racial Equality
Elliot House
10/12 Allington Street
London SW1E 5EH

Education Libraries Bulletin
University Institute of Education
Library
11-13 Ridgmount Street
London WC1E 7AE

Educational Administration
British Educational Administration
Society
Further Education Staff College
Coombe Lodge
Blagdon
Bristol BS18 6RG

Educational Media International
Council for Educational Media
Educational Foundation for Visual
Aids
National Audio Visual Aids Centre
Paxton Place
Gipsy Road
London SE27 9SR

Educational Research
National Foundation for Educational
Research
2 Oxford Road East .
Windsor
Berks

Educational Technology
140 Sylvan Avenue
Englewood Cliffs
New Jersey 07362
USA

Forum for the discussion of new
trends in education
11 Beacon Street
Lichfield WS13 7AA

Industry Newsletter
Schools Council Industry Project
160 Great Portland Street
London W1N 6LL

Instructional Innovator
Association For Educational
Communications and Technology
1126 Sixteenth St NW
Washington DC 20036
USA

Journal of Curriculum Studies
Taylor and Francis
4 John Street
London WC1N 2ET

*Journal of Educational Television and
other media*
Educational Television Association
86 Micklegate
York YO1 1JZ

*Journal of Multilingual and
Multicultural Development*
4 Bellevue Mansions
Clevedon
Avon BS21 7NU

*Library and Information Science
Abstracts (LISA)*
Library Association
7 Ridgmount Street
London WC1E 7AE

Library Association Record (LAR)
Library Association
7 Ridgmount Street
London WC1E 7AE

Library Review
30 Clydeholm Road
Glasgow G14 0BJ

Media Project News
The Volunteer Centre
29 Lower Kings Road
Berkhamsted
Herts HP4 2AB

Multiracial Education
National Association for Multiracial
Education
Midlands Road Centre
19 Midlands Road
Walsall
W. Midlands

OLS News
Council for Educational Technology
3 Devonshire Street
London W1N 2BA

Reprographics Quarterly
National Reprographic Centre for
Documentation
Hatfield Polytechnic
Bayfordsbury
Hertford SG13 8LD

School Librarian
School Library Association
Victoria House
29-31 George Street
Oxford OX1 2AY

School Technology
National Centre for School
Technology
Trent Polytechnic
Burton Street
Nottingham NG1 4BU

Schools Council Newsletter
Schools Council
160 Great Portland Street
London W1N 6LL

Secondary Education
National Union of Teachers
Hamilton House
Mabledon Place
London WC1H 9BH

Special Programmes News
Manpower Services Commission
Selkirk House
166 High Holborn
London WC1V 6PB

Studies in Adult Education
National Institute of Adult Education
19b De Montfort Street
Leicester LE1 7GE

Teaching at a distance
Open University
Milton Keynes MK7 6AA

Times Educational Supplement
Times Newspapers
PO Box 7
200 Grays Inn Road
London WC1X 8EZ

Times Higher Education
Times Newspapers
PO Box 7
200 Grays Inn Road
London WC1X 8EZ

Times Literary Supplement
Times Newspapers
PO Box 7
200 Grays Inn Road
London WC1X 8EZ

*Unesco Journal of Information
Science*
Librarianship and Archives
Administration
UNESCO
7 Place de Fontenoy
75700 Paris
France

Vine
University of Southampton Library
Highfield
Southampton SO9 5NH

Voluntary Forum Abstracts
National Council for Voluntary
Organisations
26 Bedford Square
London WC1B 3HU

Where
Advisory Centre for Education
18 Victoria Park Square
London E2 9PB

Youth in Society
National Youth Bureau
17-23 Albion Street
Leicester LE1 6GD

● **References — a selective list of relevant books and articles**

Advisory Council for Adult and Continuing Education. *Links to Learning.* Leicester ACACE, 1979.

Bates, T. and Robinson, J. *Evaluating educational television and radio.* Milton Keynes, Open University, 1977.

Bazalgette, J. L. *School Life and Work Life.* London, Hutchinson, 1978.

Beckett, L. *Maintaining choice in the secondary curriculum.* London, CET, 1981. (Working Paper 20).

Bennett, M. *Teaching styles and pupil progress.* London, Open Books, 1976.

Beswick, N. J. *Resource Based Learning.* London, Heinemann Educational, 1977.

Birch, D. W. and Cuthbert, R. E. *Costing open learning in further education.* London, CET, 1981.

Bloom, B. S. *Taxonomy of educational objectives.* New York, McKay, 1956.

Brennan, T. *Political Education and democracy.* Cambridge, CUP, 1981.

Briault, E. *Falling roles in secondary schools,* Part 1. Windsor NFER, 1980.

Brooksbank, K. (ed.) *Educational Administration.* London Councils and Education Press, 1980.

Burgess, T. and Adams, E. *Outcome of Education*. London, MacMillan Education, 1980.

Business Education Council. *First Policy Statement*. London, BEC, 1976.

Central Policy Review Staff. *Education, Training and Industrial Performance*. London, HMSO, 1980.

Central Policy Review Staff. *Social and employment implications of microelectronics*. London, National Economic Development Council, 1978.

Coffey, J. *Development of an open learning system in further education: a report*. London, CET, 1978 (Working Paper 15).

Committee of Enquiry into the Education of Handicapped Children and Young People. *Special Educational Needs*. London, HMSO, 1978 (The Warnock Report).

A comprehensive approach to the education and training of the 16-19 age range. Forum, *25* No 1. Autumn 1982.

Council for Educational Technology. *Audio Visual Resources in Secondary Schools: their organisation and management*. London, CET, 1980.

Council for Educational Technology. *Learning Resources in Colleges: their organisation and management*. London, CET, 1981.

Council for National Academic Awards. *Libraries and related resources*. London C.N.A.A., 1977. (Working party report).

Council of Europe. *Permanent education*. Strasbourg, Council of Europe, 1970.

Davie, R., Butler, N. and Goldstein, H. *From Birth to Seven*. London, Longmans in association with the National Children's Bureau, 1972.

Davies, I. K. *Management of Learning*. Maidenhead, McGraw Hill, 1971.

Davies, T. C. *Open Learning Systems for Mature Students*. London, CET, 1978 (Working Paper 14).

Department of Education and Science. *Adult Education: A Plan for Development*. London, HMSO, 1973 (The Russell Report).

Department of Education and Science. *Aspects of Secondary Education in England*. London, HMSO, 1979.

Department of Education and Science. *A better start in working life: a consultative paper*. London, Department of Employment and Department of Industry, 1979.

Department of Education and Science. *Children and their primary schools*. London, HMSO, 1967 (The Plowden Report).

Department of Education and Science. *Costing Educational Provision for the 16-19 Age Groups*. London, DES, 1982.

Department of Education and Science. *Curricula for non-participant 16-19s*. London, DES, 1976.

Department of Education and Science. *Curriculum 11-16: A Review of Progress*. London, HMSO, 1981.

Department of Education and Science. *Education: A framework for expansion*. London, DES, 1972.

Department of Education and Science. *Education for 16-19 Year Olds.* London, DES, 1981 (The Macfarlane Report).

Department of Education and Science. *Educational Disadvantage: perspective and policies.* London, HMSO, 1975

Department of Education and Science. *Examinations 16-18: a consultative paper.* London, DES, 1980.

Department of Education and Science. *A framework for the school curriculum.* London, DES, 1980.

Department of Education and Science, HMI Series: Matters for discussion No. 11 *A View of the Curriculum.* London, HMSO, 1980.

Department of Education and Science. *Higher Education in England outside the Universities: Policy, Funding and Management.* London, DES, 1981.

Department of Education and Science. *A Language for Life.* London, HMSO, 1975 (The Bullock Report).

Department of Education and Science. *The Libraries Choice.* London, DES, 1978 (Library Information Services No. 10)

Department of Education and Science. *Local Authority arrangements for the School curriculum.* London, DES, 1979.

Department of Education and Science. *Micro-Electronics Programme — The Strategy.* London, DES, 1981.

Department of Education and Science. *A new Partnership for our Schools.* London, HMSO, 1977 (The Taylor Report).

Department of Education and Science. *Providing Educational Opportunities for 16-18 Year Olds.* London, DES, 1979.

Department of Education and Science. *The School Curriculum.* London, HMSO, March 1981.

Department of Education and Science. *Schools & Industry: A guide to schools — Industry links.* London, DES, 1979.

Department of Education and Science. *Schools and Working Life: Some initiatives.* London, HMSO, 1981.

Department of Education and Science. *Secondary School Examinations: A single system at 16 plus.* London, HMSO, 1978 Cmnd. 7368.

Department of Education and Science. *16-18: Education and Training for 16-18 year olds: a consultative paper.* London, DES, and Department of Employment, 1979.

Department of Education and Science. *Statistical Bulletin: Secondary School Library Survey.* 7/81, London, DES, May 1981.

Department of Education and Science. *Teacher education and training.* London, HMSO, 1972 (The James Report).

Department of Education and Science. *Unemployed young people, the contribution of the education service.* Circ. 10/77. London, DES, 1977.

Department of Education and Science. *Unified Vocational Preparation: a pilot approach.* London.

Department of Education and Science. *Unified Vocational Preparation: an evaluation of the pilot programme.* Windsor, NFER, 1980.

Department of Education and Science. *A View of the Curriculum.* London, DES, 1979.

Department of Employment. *A new training initiative: a programme for action.* London, HMSO, 1981, Cmnd. 8455.

Department of Industry. *Industry, Education and Management — A discussion paper.* London, Department of Industry, 1977.

Department of Industry. *Industry/Education Links — A short guide to Industry/Education Links.* London, Department of Industry, 1979.

Directory of Social Action Programmes, Berkhamsted, The Volunteer Centre, 1981.

Do You Provide Equal Educational Opportunities? A guide to good practice in the provision of equal opportunities in education. Manchester, Equal Opportunities Commission, 1981.

Donoughue, C. (ed.) *In-Service: The teacher and the school.* London, Kogan Page in association with the Open University Press, 1981.

Elliott, S. *The Disraeli Project: Dizzy questionnaire answers.* London, IBA, 1979.

Fairbairn, A. N. *The Leicestershire Plan.* London, Heinemann Educational, 1980.

Fairfax, O. and Pearce, J. *Teaching and Instruction: An annotated list of resources for tutor and trainees.* London, CET, 1980.

Fernig, L. R. *The place of information in educational development.* London, HMSO, 1980.

Fielden, J. and Pearson, P. K. *Cost of Learning with Computers.* London, CET, 1978.

Fogelman, K. *Britain's 16 Year Olds.* London, National Children's Bureau, 1976.

Freeman, R. *Flexistudy: some questions answered.* Cambridge, NEC, 1981.

Further Education Curriculum Review and Development Unit. *Active Learning: a register of experimental and participatory learning, parts 1 & 2,* London, FECRADU, 1979.

Further Education Curriculum Review and Development Unit. *A basis for choice — report of a study group on post 16 pre-employment courses.* London, FECRADU, 1979.

Further Education Curriculum Review and Development Unit. *A basis for choice: resources guide.* London, FECRADU, 1981.

Further Education Curriculum Review and Development Unit. *Beyond Coping — some approaches to social education.* London, FECRADU, 1980.

Further Education Curriculum Review and Development Unit. *Curriculum Control: a review of major styles of curriculum design in FE.* London, FECRADU, 1981.

Further Education Curriculum Review and Development Unit. *Developing Social and Life Skills: Strategies for tutors.* London, FECRADU, 1980.

Further Education Curriculum Review and Development Unit. *Experience,*

Reflection, Learning. London, FECRADU, 1980.

Further Education Curriculum Review and Development Unit. *Loud and Clear? Summary of a study of curriculum dissemination in further and higher education.* London, FECRADU, 1980.

Further Education Curriculum Review and Development Unit. *17+: a new pre-vocational qualification.* London, FECRADU, 1982.

Further Education Curriculum Review and Development Unit. *Signposts: a map of 16-19 educational provision.* London, FECRADU, 1981.

Further Education Curriculum Review and Development Unit. *Stretching the System.* FECRADU, 1982.

Further Education Curriculum Review and Development Unit. *Supporting YOP: Suggestions for colleges involved in the Youth Opportunities Programme.* London, FECRADU, 1979.

Further Education Curriculum Review and Development Unit. *Transition and Access: a review of low-level FE courses in the ILEA.* FECRADU, 1981.

Further Education Curriculum Review and Development Unit. *Vocational Preparation.* London, FECRADU, 1981.

The future development of libraries and information services. London, HMSO, 1982. (DES Library information series No. 12).

Gagne, R. *The conditions of learning.* 3rd Rev Ed. New York, Holt, Reinehart and Winston, 1977.

Gains, D. 'Libraries and other information sources for open university students on higher level courses in 1976' in *Teaching at a Distance.* (11) May 1978, pp 65-69.

Haigh, R. W., Gerber, G. and Byrne, R. B. (eds) *Communications in the Twenty First Century.* Chichester, Wiley, 1981.

Harris, N. D. C. *Preparing educational materials.* London, Croom Helm, 1979.

Hayes, J., *Occupational perceptions and occupational information.* London Institute of Careers Officers, 1971.

Hicks, W. and Tillen, A. *Developing multi-media libraries.* New York, Bowker, 1970.

Hicks, W. and Tillen, A. *Managing multi-media libraries.* New York, Bowker, 1977.

Hills, P. (ed.) *The future of the printed word.* London, Pinter, 1980.

Hills, P. (ed.) *Trends in information transfer.* London, Pinter, 1982.

Holmberg. B. *Distance education.* London, Kogan Page, 1977.

Holt, M. *The Tertiary Sector.* London, Hodder and Stoughton, 1980.

Hooper, R. and Toye, I. (eds) *Computer assisted learning in the United Kingdom — some case studies.* London, CET, 1975.

Horder, A. *Video discs — their application to information storage and retrieval.* 2nd ed. Hertford, NRCD, 1981.

Houghton, V. and Richardson, K. *Recurrent education: a plea for lifelong learning.* London, Ward Lock Educational in association with the Association for Recurrent Education, 1974.

Independent Broadcasting Authority, *Television and Radio 1980: a guide to independent television and local radio.* London, IBA, 1980.

Information storage and retrieval in the British Library service. London, HMSO, 1980 (House of Commons Paper 409-1).

Information Technology and Education. Milton Keynes, Open University, 1982.

International Yearbook of Educational and Instructional Technology, 1980/81. London, Kogan Page, 1980.

Jamieson, I. and Lightfoot, M. *Schools and Industry.* London, Methuen Educational, 1982.

Jones, R. *Micro-computers in the primary school.* London, CET, 1982.

Kennerley, P. *Running a school bookshop.* London, Ward Lock Educational, 1978.

Lewis, R. *How to write self-study materials.* London, CET, 1981 (Guidelines 10).

Library Association: School Libraries Group. *The micro-electronics revolution and its implication for the School Library.* London, SLG, 1982.

Little, A. and Wiley, R. *Multi-ethnic education: the way forward.* London, Schools Council, 1981 (Schools Council pamphlet 18).

Loriac, C. and Weiss, M. *Communication and Social skills.* London, Wheaton/ Schools Council, 1981.

Luckham, B. *The library in Society.* London, Library Association, 1971.

Lunzer, E. and Gardner, K. (eds) *The effective use of reading.* Heinemann Educational Books for the Schools Council, 1979.

MacDonald, B. and May, K. M. *Broadcasting: a selected bibliography.* London, IBA, 1981.

McKenzie, N. et al *Open Learning.* Paris, UNESCO, 1975.

Maddison, A. *Micro-computers in the Classroom.* London, Hodder & Stoughton, 1982.

Mandelson, P. *Broadcasting and Youth.* London, Gulbenkian Foundation, 1980.

Manpower Services Commission, *A new training initiative.* London, MSC, 1981.

Manpower Services Commission. *An 'Open Tech' Programme: to help meet adult training and retraining needs at technician and related levels. A consultative document.* London, MSC, 1981.

Manpower Services Commission. *Outlook on Training: review of Employment and Training Act 1973.* London, MSC, 1980.

Manpower Services Commission. *Review of the first year of special programmes.* London, MSC, 1979.

Manpower Services Commission. *Young People and Work.* London, MSC, 1978 (The Holland Report).

Manpower Services Commission. *The Youth Opportunities Commission and the Local Authority.* London, MSC, 1981.

Marland, M. *Education for the Inner City.* London, Heinemann Educational, 1980.

Midwinter, E. *Priority Education.* Harmondsworth, Penguin, 1972.

Midwinter, E. *Recurrent Education. A national service for all ages at all times.*

Milner, P. *Counselling in Education.* 36, Park Vista, London SE10 9LZ.

Ministry of Education: Central Advisory Council for Education (England). 15-18. Vol. 1. Report Vol. 2. Statistics. London, HMSO, 1959. (The Crowther Report).

Ministry of Education: Central Advisory Council for Education (England). *Half our Future.* London, HMSO, 1963 (The Newsom Report).

Morby, G. and Kempson, E. *Knowhow: a guide to information, training and campaigning materials for information and advice workers.* London, Community Information Project, c/o Library Association, 1979.

Morgan, E. *Microprocessors — a short introduction.* London, Department of Industry, 1980.

National Association of Teachers in Future and Higher Education. *Education and Training for the 16-19's: a discussion paper.* London, NATFHE, 1979.

National Union of Teachers. *Examining at 16+: the case for a common system.* London, NUT, 1978.

A New Partnership for our Schools. London, HMSO, 1977 (Report of the Taylor Committee).

Pearson, P. K. *Costs of Education in the United Kingdom.* London, CET, 1977.

Percy, K. A. and Willett, I. H. (eds) *Librarians and the future of adult education.* Lancaster, University of Lancaster, 1981 (Series on Adult Education 4).

Policy Studies Institute. *Policy and Practice in the Multi-Racial City.* London, PSI, 1981.

Report of the Committee on Continuing Education Under the Chairmanship of Sir Peter Venables. Milton Keynes, Open University, 1976 (The Venables Report).

Richardson, E. *The Teacher, the School and the task of Management.* London, Heinemann Educational, 1973.

Rogers, C. R. *Freedom to Learn.* New York, Merrill, Columbus, 1969.

Rogers, J. and Groombridge, B. *Right to Learn: the case for adult equality.* London, Arrow, 1976.

Rowntree, D. *Educational Technology in curriculum development.* London, Harper & Row, 1974.

Royal Society of Arts, *Office technology: the implications for education and training in the 1980s.* London, RSA, 1981.

Rubber and Plastics Processing Industry Training Board. *Work and Learning: proposals for a national scheme for 16-18 year olds at work.* London, R & PPITB, 1978.

Rubber and Plastics Processing Industry Training Board. *School Curricula for a changing World: second report of the study group on the education/training of young people.* London, R & PPITB, 1976.

Rubber and Plastics Processing Industry Training Board. *Third report of the study group on the education/training of young people.* London, R & PPITB,

1978.

Rushby, N. *Selected readings in computer based learning*. London, Kogan Page, 1981.

Rutter, M. *Fifteen thousand hours*. London, Open Books, 1979.

Rutter, M. and Madge, N. *Cycles of disadvantage*. London, Heinemann Educational, 1976.

Schools Council. *CEE: proposals for a new examination*. London, Evans/ Methuen, 1975.

Schools Council. *Choosing a curriculum for the young school leaver*. London, Evans/Methuen Educational, 1971 (Working Paper 33).

Schools Council. *Closer links between teachers and industry and commerce*. London, Schools Council, 1966 (Working Paper 7).

Schools Council. *A common system of examining at 16+*. London, Evans/ Methuen Educational, 1971 (Examination Bulletin 23).

Schools Council. *Cross'd with Adversity: the education of socially disadvantaged children in secondary schools*. London, Evans/Methuen Educational, 1970 (Working Paper 27).

Schools Council. *Education for a multi-racial society: Curriculum and context 5-13*. London, Schools Council, 1981.

Schools Council. *Examinations at 18 plus: Report on the N and F debate*. London, Methuen Educational, 1980 (Schools Council Working Paper 66).

Schools Council. *General Studies 16-18*. London, Schools Council, 1969 (Schools Council Working Paper 25).

Schools Council. *Information skills in the secondary curriculum*. London, Methuen Educational, 1981 (Schools Council Curriculum Bulletin 9).

Schools Council. *The practical curriculum*. London, Evans/Methuen, 1981 (Schools Council Working Paper 70).

Schools Council. *Secondary examinations post 16: a programme of improvement*. London, Schools Council, 1980.

Schools Council. *16-19 Growth and Response. 1 Curriculum bases*. Evans/ Methuen Educational, 1972 (Working Paper 45).

Schools Council. *16-19 Growth and Response. Examination Structure*. London, Evans/Methuen Educational, 1973 (Working Paper 46).

Schools Council. *Sixth Form curriculum and examinations*. London, HMSO, 1965 (Working Paper 5).

Scottish Council for Educational Technology. *A guide to distance (open) learning opportunities for people in Scotland*. Glasgow, SCET, 1981.

Sharp, J. *Open School*. London, Dent, 1973.

Shipman, M. *Inside a curriculum project*. London, Methuen, 1974.

Simon, M. *Youth into Industry*. London, National Youth Bureau, 1977.

Spencer, D. *Thinking about open learning systems*. London, CET, 1980 (Working Paper 19).

Stenhouse, L. *An introduction to curriculum research and development*.

London, Heinemann Educational, 1975.

Technician Education Council. *Policy Statement.* London, TEC, 1974.

Thomason, N. V. (ed.) *The library media specialist in curriculum development.* Scarecrow, 1981.

Thompson, V. *Prestel and education: a report of a one-year trial.* London, CET, 1981.

Tough, A. *The adults learning project: a fresh approach to theory and practice in adult learning.* Toronto, Ontario Institute for Studies in Education, 1971.

Towards a Wider Use. Association of County Councils. London, nd.

Watmore, G. *The modern news library.* London, Library Association, 1978.

Weir, A. D. and Nolan, F. S. *Glad to be out?* Glasgow, Scottish Council for Research in Education, 1977.

West Indian Children in our Schools. Interim report of the Committee of Inquiry into the Education of Children from Ethnic Minority Groups. London, HMSO, 1981 (The Rampton Report).

Whitehouse, P. *Handbook of classroom management for independent learning.* Bristol, Resources for Learning Development Unit, nd.

Willis, N. (ed.) *Teaching and learning support services: 1 Higher Education; 2 Further Education; 3 Secondary comprehensive, Middle and Primary schools.* London, CET, 1981.

Wilson, T. D. 'Learning at a distance and library use: open university students and libraries'. in *Libri* 28 (4), 1978 pp. 270-280.

Winsbury, R. *Viewdata in action: a comparative study of Prestel.* London, New York, McGraw, Hill, 1981.

Wright, J. *Learning to learn in higher education.* London, Croom Helm, 1982.

Yardley, A. and Swain, H. *Community schools in practice.* London, Home and School Council Publications, 1980.

York, D. M. *Patterns of teaching.* London, CET, 1981.

- Be informed about major changes which take place nationally (including educational changes which include teacher training at the initial and in-service stages). These can and do affect methodology and so the use of resources. (Union contributions to change factors are also important to note.)

- Be informed about major reports which will affect resources e.g. changes in curricular content and organisation. Make sure that the Library can cope with resultant changes in terms of facilities, organisation and stock. (The major recommendations of most reports are contained in the conclusions — easily readable.)

- Extract crucial factors and ideas and base future plans round these factors.

- Establish any relevant committees or working parties to carry out recommendations if they are directly geared to the library, or join in any other groups which are set up and which relate to the work of the library. Try and be involved in utilising all existing expertise within the school or college. If directly in charge of any such group, establish a planning programme, giving detailed plans, a time scale, and list of objectives as otherwise good will becomes dissipated.

- Assess stock in the light of reports, such as the Rampton Report, RSA Reports, the Holland Report and the publications of the Further Education Unit.

- Be prepared to change and alter services to cope with changes in teaching and learning patterns, and subsequent organisational change within the establishment. (Structural constraint and curricular constraints must be considered.)

- Periodically check what is happening in the field of research (in education and librarianship). This gives information on current trends and thinking so that the individual libraries can reflect national trends and concerns.

3 Changing patterns of provision: curricular planning and organisation

The effects that educational, social and economic forces have had upon education and, in particular, changes in teaching and learning patterns, such as the current emphasis on project work, individualised learning, and workshop activities, have in turn affected the pattern of provision (curriculum organisation) which was previously mainly school and college based. Rapidly falling rolls, the need to reassess the break in education at sixteen plus, an increase in post-sixteen unemployment, non-examinable courses, and now an increase in those 'staying on' in education as an alternative to the dole queue have all contributed to these changes. A brief look at these organisational changes is sufficient, but they are relevant, both in terms of career patterns for librarians, and in awareness of pressures, so that libraries can react if and when the parent institution changes, modifies, merges or is reborn in another pattern. In all cases the wide range of courses available and differing ways of teaching and learning ('operational and intellectual levels') have to be reflected in library stocks and organisation.

The 'traditional' sixth form structure

This caters now for an increasingly wide range of students, including those who are taking non-examinable courses (the 'new' sixth), and those taking the existing A level courses. The organisational pattern at sixth form level varies in differing parts of the country, but some basic patterns can be isolated:

(a) sixth forms as part of an 'all through' school, either grammar or comprehensive;
(b) as the upper tier of a two tier comprehensive;
(c) as part of a local consortium, linking several schools (can be called the 'mushroom' type);
(d) forming part of a short course comprehensive leading to a sixth form college;
(e) forming the upper tier of primary, middle and senior school provision;
(f) part of or forming a sixth form 'centre' (peculiar to the ILEA).

Sixth form colleges

These provide alternative provision to school at sixteen-plus. They are comparatively recent, most have an open access policy and offer a wide range of courses, ranging from City and Guilds to A levels. Although they operate under school regulations, they have an 'adult' atmosphere, and offer a wide choice of options. Operating under school regulations acts as a constraint in staffing matters, as school library 'standards' (even if applied) are woefully inadequate. At present there are almost 100 colleges in the United Kingdom, and they are increasing in popularity.

Further education colleges

These also offer alternative provision to school based courses, and have a wide range of options and an equally wide range of attendance patterns. It is not only the impact and effect of external forces in the early 1980s which have affected the courses offered, but also links with local schools, Industrial Training Boards, local industry and the MSC, and the YOP (the TOPS and UVP programmes), all impinging on and altering the organisation and use of resources. Further Education has always responded to change, and this picture will alter yet again with further concentration on the education and training of the post-sixteen age group, which many organisations and unions think should be seen as a complete organic unit, linking education and training under one umbrella. All this will affect library organisation at both school and college level. A clearer understanding of needs in all types of institution, leading to an increase in the joint use of resources, will become increasingly important. With these changes will also come demands for in-service training for staff (both teaching staff and librarians) to cope with new demands.

Tertiary colleges

These colleges are located in areas which previously offered a choice of school and sixth form provision, and which have now rationalised and combined all provision within one establishment. The majority have an open access policy, and so again offer a wide range of courses at a variety of levels and with a variety of attendance patterns. They operate under FE regulations and as they can offer such a wide range of subjects can also combine vocational and academic courses, thus catering for individual student needs. The majority maintain close links with their feeder schools, and provide facilities and courses for the local community, with library implications for both stock and services. Many are also involved in programmes of 'open learning', breaking down previous administrative barriers, and so providing access for the community to educational facilities, again including libraries and resources. The whole concept of the 'open' college in relation to open learning is typified by the activities of Nelson and Colne College, in co-operation with Lancaster University and Preston Polytechnic, to try and alter the constrictions of the A level route to higher education. The work of the National Extension College has also been very influential in this area, both in its involvement with other agencies and in the production of materials.

Link/bridging courses

There is wide variety in local practice, but these courses are intended to bridge activities between school and post-school institutions, and between school/college and industry. Basically such courses, regardless of organisation, are concerned with the problems of the transition from school to work. There are inevitably problems over timetabling and the planning of resources, but these courses are localised efforts to provide alternative provision which will close the gap between existing provision, and to concentrate particularly on low academic achievers. It is important that all staff involved in any of these schemes are fully aware of local developments in both industrial and educational areas, and the librarian is important here as an information agency.

Leading on from these institutional changes are others which are operating on a wider sphere, and the open college mentioned earlier is one part of an open learning system, which in turn has evolved from the awareness of educators of a need to provide opportunities for recurrent and continuing education — 'éducation permanente'. Some of these activities are rather more public library based than others, such as the adult independent learner concept, while those based on existing college provision are part of open learning systems, which can be either college (or school) based, locally based, (home and college) or entirely distance based (such as the Open University).

At the core of both these concepts lies an awareness of the need to provide and support the individual with resources, and to move away from the rigidities of institutionalised provision. Librarians in the further education and tertiary sectors are particularly liable to be involved in these developments (including Flexistudy and the use of National Extension College materials) but with the current emphasis on the co-operative use of resources, and the effective use of plant and resources, schools may also be involved. The community use of plant and resources may well develop as a result of the blurring of these boundaries. It will be increasingly important for libraries and librarians to provide counselling, information, and referral services, with implications both for the initial and in-service training of librarians. Librarians should be able to act as animators and guides to a wide range of other services, using their information expertise and concern for the user, and they could and should provide an effective channel for both resources and information — open learning systems depend on such channels.

Other changes include the provision of institution based courses for those returning to education, or attending college for the first time as mature students. These courses are not 'open' in the sense that they are free of traditional constraints, but do cater for the learning needs of particular groups of students, and so library stocks and services are again very important. The 'New Opportunities Courses for Women', 'Fresh Horizons' and 'Second Chance' courses mentioned earlier are examples of innovation in this area, and illustrate patterns of change. Local learning groups, both formal in concept, such as the WEA, and informal, such as those based on 'self-help' principles, may also utilise library resources.

changing patterns of provision

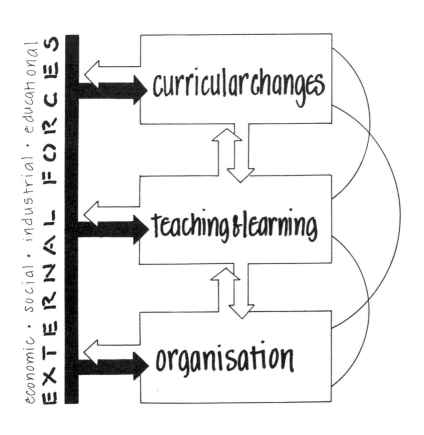

Association for Liberal Education
Secretary
Mid-Kent College of Further and
Higher Education
City Way
Rochester
Kent

Association of Colleges of Further
and Higher Education
Secretary — ACFHE
Sheffield City Polytechnic
Pond Street
Sheffield S1 1WB

Association of Head Mistresses
29 Gordon Square
London WC1H 0PS

Association of Principals of Colleges
East Herts College
Turnford
Broxbourne
Herts EN10 6AF

Association of Vice Principals of
Colleges
Honorary Secretary
Harrow College of Higher Education
Northwick Park
Harrow
Middlesex HA1 3TP

General Studies Association
75 Park Road
Sutton Coldfield B73 6BT

Head Masters Conference
29 Gordon Square
London WC1H 0PS

Library Association
Colleges of Further and Higher
Education Group
Library Association
7 Ridgmount Street
London WC1E 7AE

National Association of Head
Teachers
41-3 Boltro Road
Haywards Heath
Sussex RH16 1BJ

National Association of Teachers in
Further and Higher Education
Hamilton House
Mabledon Place
London WC1H 9BH

Open College Federation
Details: Derek Crossland
Nelson and Colne College
Scotland Road
Nelson BB9 7YT

Open Learning Federation
Nye Rowlands
Fielden Park College
Barlow Moor Road
West Didsbury
Manchester M20

Secondary Heads Association
Gordon House
29 Gordon Square
London WC1H 0PS

Sixth Form College Library Group
c/o Secretary
Farnham College Library
Morley Road
Farnham
Surrey GU9 8LU

Standing Conference of Sixth Form &
Tertiary Colleges
Joint Standing Conference Secretary
Greenhead College
Huddersfield
West Yorkshire HD1 4ES

Tertiary College Panel
c/o Bridgwater College
Broadway
Bridgwater
Somerset TA6 5HW

● **Journals — a selective list**

BEC News
Business Education Council
Berkshire House
168-173 High Holborn
London WC1V 7AG

Coombe Lodge Reports
Further Education Staff College
Coombe Lodge
Blagdon
Bristol BS18 6RG

Educa
Guildford Educational Services Ltd
164 High Street
Guildford
Surrey GU1 3HW

Education
Longmans
Fourth Avenue
Harlow
Essex

Further Education Unit — Newsletter
Elizabeth House
York Road
London SE1 7PH

NATFHE Journal
NATFHE
Hamilton House
Mabledon Place
London WC1H 9BH

OLS News
CET
3 Devonshire Street
London W1N 2BA

Open Learning Federation Newsletter
Peter Marshall
Barnet College
Wood Street
Barnet
Herts

TEC News
Technicians Education Council
Central House
Upper Woburn Place
London WC1H 0HH

Times Educational Supplement
Times Newspapers
P.O. Box 7
Grays Inn Road
London WC1X 8EZ

● References — a selective list of relevant books, reports and articles

Briault, E. and Smith, F. *Falling Rolls in Secondary Schools.* Part 1. Windsor, NFER, 1980.

Buckle, E. et al. *The Young Student in Further Education and the Sixth Form.* Hatfield, Herts, 1977.

Coffey, J. *Development of an Open Learning System for Further Education.* London, CET, 1978. (Working Paper 15).

Dean J. et al. *The Sixth Form and its Alternatives.* Windsor, NFER, 1979.

Dean, J. and Choppin, B. *Educational Provision 16-19.* Windsor, NFER, 1977.

Department of Education and Science. *The Organisation of Secondary Education.* Circ. 10/65. London, DES, 1965.

Department of Education and Science. *Sixth Form Colleges in 1980.* London, DES, 1980.

Education for 16-19 Year Olds. London, DES, 1980. (Macfarlane Report).

Fogelman, K. *Leaving the Sixth Form.* Windsor, NFER, 1972.

Holt, M. *The Tertiary Sector.* London, Hodder and Stoughton, 1980.

King, E. J., Moor, C. H. and Mundy, J. A. *Post-compulsory education: a new analysis in Western Europe.* London, Sage Publications, 1974.

King, R. *School and College: Studies of post-sixteen education.* London, Routledge and Kegan Paul, 1976.

Lewis, R. *How to Tutor in an Open Learning Scheme: Group study version.* London, CET, 1981.

Library Association. *Sixth Form College Libraries.* (LA Statement) LAR 81 (8) August, 1979. p. 319.

MacFarlane, E. *Sixth Form Colleges.* London, Heinemann Educational, 1978.

National Association of Teachers in Further and Higher Education. *College Libraries policy statement.* London, NATFHE, 1982.

National Association of Teachers in Further and Higher Education. *Education and Training for the 16-19s:* a discussion paper. London, NATFHE, 1979.

Peterson, A. D. A. *The Future of the Sixth Form.* London, Routledge and Kegan Paul, 1978.

Sixth Form College Libraries: an insight. Hornchurch, Ian Hendry Publications Ltd, 1982.

Vincent, D. and Dean, J. *One Year Courses in Colleges & Sixth Forms.* Windsor, NFER, 1977.

Watkins, P. *The sixth form college in practice.* London, Edward Arnold, 1983.

Planning pointers

● Read committee reports, and be informed of changes at a national level in curriculum organisation and re-organisation.

● Understand why these changes are taking place and plan for the individual school or college contribution.

● Relate changes to library practice and provision. Support change with appropriate resource planning and provision.

● Get involved in any committees or working parties that are involved in such changes, and contribute positively to them.

● Contribute to the management of change, not to the prevention of change.

Part 2
WHAT RESOURCES?
How to plan
for provision

4   How to plan for resource provision: contextual frameworks

When planning a new library, extending existing services, or planning a merger, the framework of support (and constraint) at local levels must be identified as a first step in the process. Based on this framework, planning for the users, for the management and organisation of resources (service needs), staffing levels, and then the adoption of personal strategies, all follow logically within this pattern.

The local authority structure and influence (County, Borough, Metropolitan Area etc.)

Level 1 (General: authority level)

Within this broad framework there are other factors which also have to be considered in the preliminary planning stages of a school/college library service, both by the individual librarian responsible for the service point, and by those involved in library planning and provision at local authority level. These factors are important as they relate to and in turn determine staffing structures, budgets, procedures, communication and formal and informal relationships.

It is important to distinguish between advisory and executive services, and the relationship of each to each other and to the total local authority service. Structures vary enormously, as do the executive 'heads' under which library services are placed, ranging from education services to leisure services to chief executives. A clear understanding of the hierarchy and the basic executive departments and their areas of responsibility is crucial, particularly of those departments that relate to financial control, staffing standards, conditions of service and pay, planning and building, in-service training and staff development, as working with and sending information to the correct people at the correct time not only saves mistakes and delays, but builds up confidence in a potential and actual library service. This is an obvious but essential element in planning.

It is relatively easy to identify the basic executive departments and obtain information on their services, but it is also important to identify the services which may be purely advisory or which may have several functions. Those which relate to libraries may well be clearly identifiable, and then their area of responsibility and support noted. This is important, as they will in turn work with and identify with some of the executive departments who must be involved in initial planning, such as planning and architectural departments. It is also important to be aware of umbrella executive and advisory services in the educational area, as these will of course influence the planning of library services. Again some may be advisory and some may be executive, while others may have a dual or linked role, depending on the main structure of the authority. These include, for example, curriculum support and development through the authority's inspectors and advisers (at all levels), production services (in-house materials) the careers and counselling services, museum services, adult education, and community services in the widest sense. They all relate in a variety of ways to each other, and all will, directly or indirectly, affect the library services.

If these services are seen as a local response to the national changes outlined earlier, then their relevance to the library service is clear. Increasingly national change factors will force local authorities to react with increasing speed (as in the case of providing courses for the non-academic, and in the establishment of tertiary colleges, for example). Library services will then also have to react quickly and be seen to be flexible and to respond to the needs of the local community. In the current economic and social climate it will become increasingly important for everyone in the community to have equal access to information and to educational facilities, for both professional and personal enrichment.

Level 2 (Specific: library services)

This can be seen as the establishment of major areas of responsibility at authority level relating to educational services in the broad sense (if applicable), and to library services as a discrete part of these, or to library services as a discrete part of any other administrative structure. This delineation should also be carried out at the very local level, relating a service point in one establishment to the library support services which are available from the authority. This is to determine need, plan relevant services, establish a reasonable staffing structure, prevent duplication of services, and exploit all support services available within the existing structure.

It is important to find out what system (or systems) are available for previewing, supplying, purchasing and producing materials. This may include centralised bibliographical services (helping standardisation), and support for subject specialisms, linking to particular centres or establishments. It is necessary to establish the range of these services in relation to pupil and student abilities. These will help in interlending and co-operation. The availability of reviewing services and access to expensive reviewing journals and bibliographical tools, plus review copies, should also be established. Any services which relate to particular group and community needs should also be checked (mother-tongue materials, reading schemes, films, software etc.), again to help plan stock, give support when and where necessary and avoid duplication. Basic support services such as interlending schemes, loans from specialist collections of all sorts, block loans, project loans, supplementary stock supplements and photocopying services should be checked. The production facilities for in-house materials are also important, and can be centrally or locally carried out. These are important, and so is the costing of such services. It is also important to determine who carries the costs relating to the supply and maintenance of furnishings and equipment. The maintenance of equipment may be at a central or local level, but central or local support has implications for technical and support staff in the planning stages.

The allocation of funding is crucial and relates both to the library services and to individual schools and colleges. Funding may be centrally controlled or may vary within each school and college, but who has control, and how the budget is administered are vital facts. This control can range from committee decisions to personal (Head or Principal) decisions, working to authority standards, and a variety of others, but it is important to know how this is carried out and how it relates to any centralised procedures or support.

Level 3 (Specific school or college structure)

It is important to understand the policies and procedures of the individual school or college so that they form a framework for library plans and activities. Within each establishment the framework can then be used for the development of the library resources centre — it is counter productive to work at a tangent or in opposition to the mainstream of ideas. The policies of the establishment are related in turn to local and national trends, but are also specific, and relate to the ability range of students, particularly areas of concern or speciality, concentration on vocational or exam oriented courses, and links with other institutions. From these policies emerges a structure which supports them, and then an organisational structure which allows the policies to be reflected. Curriculum planning and curriculum organisation have in turn to be carried out through these channels. In turn teaching patterns are established, with implications for resource provision use and evaluation. Once this skeleton has been isolated, it becomes much easier to participate in the life of the school in a realistic and meaningful way.

Within the parameters of the school or college, the librarian has to plan and provide opportunities for leadership, working decisions, coping with inter-personal relationships, and presenting him or herself as an effective Head of a department within the educational and organisational context of the school or college.

school or college contexts

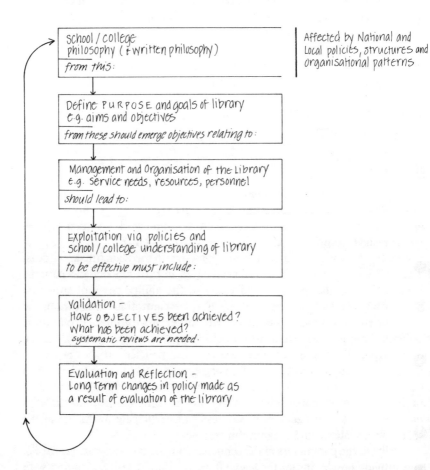

School / college
philosophy (& written philosophy)
from this:

Affected by National and Local policies, structures and organisational patterns

Define PURPOSE and goals of library
e.g. aims and objectives
from these should emerge objectives relating to:

Management and Organisation of the Library
e.g. service needs, resources, personnel
should lead to:

Exploitation via policies and
school / college understanding of library
to be effective must include:

Validation –
Have OBJECTIVES been achieved?
What has been achieved?
systematic reviews are needed.

Evaluation and Reflection –
Long term changes in policy made as
a result of evaluation of the library

Planning pointers

Level 1

- Check local authority structure and hierarchy and obtain a guide to personnel and departments. Establish the place of the library services in the structure.

- Check where and how financial control is exercised. What standards and/or limits are in force? What emergency funding is available? What is the extent of central control and local autonomy?

- Check what local general services are available (e.g. training facilities, information services etc.) and any costing.

- Check the extent (and formality) of support for curriculum change at Inspectoral and Adviser level.

- Check the availability and costs of any related services, such as the provision of hardware, software, production facilities, and any other resource materials. Check the extent of centralised services, shared services (e.g. local cooperation) and individual establishment services.

Level 2

- Check what library support services are available and where. These tend to fall into two groupings — senior staffing support (advisory and/or executive) and service support.

- Find out the names of the personnel involved and their areas of responsibility.

- Check if there are any special areas of responsibility, such as staffing, finance, or services, for particular groups of users.

- Find out all the details of the services (including all specialist services and collections of materials in all formats) which are available, and any conditions or costs relating to their use.

- Make these details available within the school/college.

Level 3

- Find out the historical background of the school/college. Does it operate under school or FE regulations?

- What is its policy? Is it written down?

- Check the admissions policy and the catchment area (these will be your target users).

- Find out how the structure is organised — by department or faculty or year, etc.

- Find out how the library and the librarian relate to this structure.

- Find out how and where finance is allocated.

- Check main courses offered and patterns of attendance (through departments).

- File a copy of all the major syllabuses.

- How does communication work? Is there a committee structure?

- Find out if there are any special committees or groups of specialists concerned with particular local needs.

- Find out what extra curricular activities take place, both educational and socially.

FINALLY

- When planning make sure that both the proposed plans (and any existing services) are considered in relation to national standards, and also other acknowledged 'good practice'. This helps to determine a realistic service level, and avoid either complacency or unrealistic requests.

5   Planning for the users

Any planned services will of course reflect and relate to the needs of the users. These will be determined to some extent by external forces of change, by local and institutional policies, and by the articulated needs of the users themselves.

The first group of users will be the pupils/students, and it is important to be familiar with their age and ability ranges, their background and the prevalent teaching and learning activities in their feeder schools. Other factors which should be considered include links with local higher education establishments, links with local industry, and the general pattern of progression from school to work and from school to further/higher education. The second group consists of staff and administrators, full time and part time (including specialists) and those involved in teaching practice. Their needs will be clear in relation to subject areas, organisation of courses, and the ways in which they use resource materials. Those involved in research projects or professional development courses will also have special needs. The third group of users are those in the local community, who will have access to the school/college in a variety of ways depending on local organisation. Adaptability is equally important, as routines must follow need and not constrain or determine it. The open college, flexistudy, and the use of school facilities by disabled students are all examples of the community influencing library resource provision and practice. All those who are involved in any way can be considered as users, and each group must be considered in relation to its specific needs, but also in relation to other groups of users. There are some core areas, and some overlapping areas. Having identified the target groups of users, it then becomes possible to begin to identify their information needs. These needs cover current personal and social information, future personal and social information, current curricular needs and future curricular needs. The nature of the information in relation to these contexts can then to some extent be distinguished, together with the potential role and place it has in that context. This can be extracted formally (from printed sources) and informally (orally) through the planning processes and strategies in which the librarian is involved. Other sources of advice include the local authority (inspectorate) and national research projects. The skills involved by the user in obtaining his or her own personal information requirements range from basic literacy (alphabetisation) and numeracy skills to the use of abstracts, statistics, documentation and on line bibliographical and non-bibliographical services. The extent and level of these help to determine the extent of the services required, and indicate the need for planned in-service training. This again will be necessary at a variety of levels, for staff and students, and members of the identified community.

So by considering the needs of the users, both actual and potential, decisions can be made on what to provide in the library, for whom, how, when and where. The logistics of the service and the resultant budget are then the final process in this particular planning exercise, based on information found inside the school/college.

the users

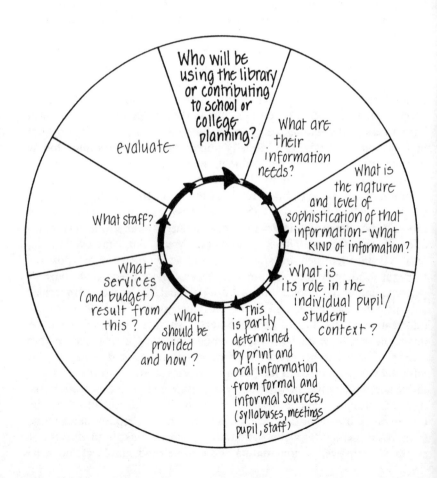

Planning pointers

- Define the parameters of the expected and perceived user groups.

- Define the information needs of these groups of users through as many sources as possible, both formal and informal.

- Include all those who are involved in school or college policies, in the widest sense.

- Plan for their needs in relation to policies and constraints which already exist, and in relation to future developments.

- Collect supporting information from authority sources, school or college sources, governors, prospectuses, and the curriculum itself.

- Provide services.

- Evaluate services.

6 Planning the management and organisation of resources

General planning

Overview leading to   (i) funding, (ii) selection, (iii) acquisition, (iv) access, organisation of space and storage, (v) production, (vi) bibliographical organisation and control.

Overview

All resources have to relate with the school curriculum, with its planning, its organisation, and teaching and learning patterns. The allocation of funds partly controls the selection of resource materials, although this must follow the identification of need, which determines decisions on levels, availability and use. The organisation and exploitation of information follow logically from planning within contexts.

Budgeting depends on the formal and informal policy decisions and structures outlined earlier, but once the librarian has been given a resource fund then management decisions have to be made over its spending. Decisions on the purchase of expensive bibliographical and reference tools, including bibliographies, directories, abstracts, microforms and statistical materials, as well as access to on-line data bases (bibliographic and subject based) will depend on the availability of these through central or local services. The librarian has to decide if each department should be given a set allocation, or if funding should be related to demand and use. Consideration should be given to the cost of basic materials in various subject areas, expensive in the science areas for example, and to the number of journals required. Patterns of use must be considered (e.g. full or part-time students in the college sector, with implications for multiple purchase of text books), and the ways in which departmental or satellite collections are or are not used. It is also important to consider the extent of in-house materials produced by departments and the extent to which they need to be supplemented (films for example). Research and professional interests have to be considered, as well as purely recreational reading.

The selection process involves the purchase of relevant journals (also to be costed), organisation of previewing, and consultation with subject specialists), organisation of previewing, and consultation with subject specialists. Central services again must be used, as well as specialist bookshops and local centres of excellence, expertise and research activities. All groups of users must be catered for in the selection process, including minority groups, subject areas, reference materials, local needs (including the community), handicapped students, and specialist areas forming part of a local network or co-operative system.

Purchasing schemes vary enormously, but are of course tied to finance. As far as possible any other services that are part of purchasing systems should be used, such as previewing, processing, central invoicing, approval schemes and specialist subject purchasing services.

Access must be linked to patterns of use within the school/college, planned and available spaces, and to policies on the use of resources — for teacher support, student use or a combination of both. Efficient storage schemes for materials are important to ensure easy access. Local co-operative schemes involving specialisms also have an effect on access, as do satellite centres, and the production of materials relates to all these factors.

The organisation of materials is based on the theory of the organisation of knowledge, its management, through applying a classification scheme and cataloguing materials, and the exploitation and use of materials.

The decisions on what classification scheme and what cataloguing code to use relate to personal preferences, training and, more important, the size of the collection, the number of users, number of staff, central support available and potential use. Note must also be taken of national as well as local developments, so that in librarianship terms schemes are correctly used, and in user terms pupils and students do not constantly have to learn how to re-use a system. The classification scheme must be applied consistently, with a catalogue which supports the user and also functions as an effective means of stock control and exploitation.

The exploitation of materials becomes increasingly important as all resources have to be fully utilised as finance becomes tighter. Any programmes which improve the pupils' understanding of information skills must be based within the curriculum and be co-operative in approach. A library skills programme produced in isolation is of little value. Details, levels, tactics and materials used will vary from school to school, but the basic principle of the full use of resources remains the same, so that they are fully maximised intellectually and personally for the institution, the subject and the individual pupil, as well as economically.

Evaluation of resources can be a quantitative or qualitative exercise. The first can be checked through available standards and statistics, and the second is much more difficult, as it relates to both quality and use. Qualitative evaluation and revision of materials includes provision for and elimination of materials in relation to changing social and economic trends — relevance is vital. To a certain extent the use made of resources is also an indication (although not the only one) of the relevance of those resources.

Funding and finance

The system of funding and allocation of finance again relates to other administrative structures, and the library cannot operate in isolation. Budgets have to relate to the wider and long term educational planning both within the school and the authority, with the added national constraints also having an effect.

Library decisions on spending again are related to the degree of central support in terms of 'subsidised' services, and access to support services, such as technical maintenance, which do not involve direct costs. They also relate to the ways in which resources are used within the schools. These determine if there is a 'central' pool of equipment and resources, or satellite collections, or a combination of both, as patterns of use will determine the allocation of departmental budgets, including the library. The way in which finance is allocated within the school is important both managerially, so that the librarian is involved in all committees which relate to finance, and organisationally, in the ways in which finance is divided under various budget heads, and the degree of flexibility ('virement') allowed. The availability and allocation of alternative funding for short term projects is also an important element.

Authority policies and patterns of spending will of course affect those within the school, and the library must plan, budget and provide information in the local context. It is possible to provide for short term and 'crisis' budgeting, but long term budget plans must derive from the library objectives and service needs.

It is necessary for the library to keep careful and accurate budget records so that funding can be monitored and evaluated. The maintenance of accurate records enables the librarian to check local provision with regional and national provision, both to ensure that standards are maintained and also to ensure the effective preparation of budgets.

As with all other policy decisions, the actual materials which are purchased are determined by the use of materials within the school and the extent of in-house productions. The library involvement in the planning, preparation and use of materials will affect the amount of money which is spent on commercially available materials including reference and bibliographical tools, as well as journals and ephemera. This involvement and the school policy on the use of resources and the extent of resource based teaching and resource based learning will also influence the amount of money spent on materials, on software and on equipment.

● Information — a selective list of relevant groups, institutes and associations

Booksellers Association
154 Buckingham Palace Road
London SW1

Chartered Institute of Public Finance
and Accountancy
1 Buckingham Place
London SW1E 6HJ

Educational Publishers Council
Publishers Association
19 Bedford Square
London WC1B 3HJ

Library Association
7 Ridgmount Street
London WC1E 7AE

National Book League
Book House
45 East Hill
Wandsworth
London SW18 2HZ

Publishers Association
19 Bedford Square
London WC1B 3JE

University, College and Professional
Publishing Council
The Publishers Association
19 Bedford Square
London WC1B 3JE

● Journals — a selective list

Bookseller
J. Whitaker & Sons Limited
12 Dyott Street
London WC1

Education
Longmans
Fourth Avenue
Harlow, Essex

LAMSAC News
Local Authority Management
Services & Computer Committee
3 Buckingham Gate
London SW1E 6JH

Library Association Record (LAR)
Library Association
7 Ridgmount Street
London WC1E 7AE

● References — a selective list of relevant books, reports and articles

British Educational Equipment Association *and* Educational Publishers Council. *School books and equipment: a spending guide for local education authorities: 1982-83.* London, BEEA and EPC, 1982.
Chartered Institute of Public Finance & Accountancy. *Education statistics, 1979-1980.* London, CIPFA, 1981.

Library Book Spending in Universities, Polytechnics and Colleges. London, National Book League, 1982.

National Book League. *Books for schools: report of a working party convened by the National Book League to consider aspects of the provision of books to schools.* London, NBL, 1979.

The supply of books to schools and colleges. London, Booksellers Association and Publishers Association, 1981. (Lady David Committee).

University College and Professional Publishing Council. *The economics of university and textbook publishing in the United Kingdom.* London, University College and Professional Publishing Council, 1982.

Planning pointers

- Determine what centralised support services (college and school) already exist, at subsidised or no costs.

- Determine patterns of use of resources in school or college, e.g., central, departmental and satellite use.

- Find out how the budget is allocated at LEA level and also variations and flexibility of allocation at school level.

- Find out how the budget is allocated within the school or college, and how decisions are made. Distinguish between committee decisions and personal decisions.

- Prepare long term and short term budgets derived from library objectives and services. Learn how to present these and argue for a reasonable budget.

- Monitor expenditure.

- Note national standards and statistics of educational resource spending to maintain school or college standards.

- Use statistics with care, but keep abreast of national developments.

Selection

Selection criteria

When selecting materials for a school library there are some clear general principles which need to be applied, regardless of the format of the items. Other criteria can be applied to distinct groups of items, including books and journals, non print materials (in all formats) and equipment. Micro computers and the relevant software programmes form another category which, although discrete in itself, also overlaps with other formats. The other set of information carriers, on-line data bases, both bibliographical and non-bibliographical also form discrete groups on their own, while also overlapping the other groups to some extent. All will be selected, purchased and used at some time for library use, with a varying degree of involvement by the librarian, and so the application of any such criteria by the librarian is important, particularly so in relation to the costs involved. The application of criteria springs from a close liaison with the teaching staff, through methods of selection, and through the integration of the librarian into the structure of the school or college.

General criteria

General criteria relate to and are determined by 'natural' factors and constraints, and can be both positive and negative. Many of them stem from and are decided by some of the basic planning decisions, and the selection criteria will of course have to relate to and enrich school policies and educational goals, the users of the library, curricular content and organisation, teaching contexts (including size of classes, resources involved, ability levels and subject areas, the acquisition of specific skills) and the professional needs of teaching staff. Criteria also relate to the structuring of materials, particularly in 'package' format, as these may or may not conform to the policies and practices within the school. The area in which the school is located may also help determine selection policies. This is particularly so in Educational Priority Areas, those with large ethnic communities, or other special social characteristics.

It is also important to select materials in relation to curriculum content and innovation, taking advice from those directly involved, such as inspectors and advisers, and also taking note of new national trends in this area. Local and in-house materials may either supplement or replace commercial items, but their role and availability must be considered.

National and international changes in the publication and production of information and resources will also affect and change criteria. The growth of electronic data base publishing (Lexis etc.) will influence reference materials purchased, and therefore access by schools to expensive reference items. The relevance of teletext (Prestel etc.) will influence the number and range of reference books available, affecting selection both at school and college level. The speed of producing materials, using word processors for example, will affect local curriculum support and possibly lead to the purchase of fewer commercial items.

More detailed criteria will stem from a consideration of the physical format of items — e.g. is expensive equipment already in stock, can the materials be more cheaply produced in-house, is the quality good, is advice available on how and when to use the materials? Many items in all formats are advertised as new but are in fact reconstituted packages, and this physical aspect needs consideration. The organisation of material in relation to its intended teaching and learning uses is also important, and the sequencing of information and the language used (its range and style) is another important facet of this intended use. The way in which the information which has been included is designed and presented also needs to be considered. The problem of quality versus quantity is also a decision which has to be taken, and in some cases the criterion of quality may over-rule that of quantity (six small items or one expensive reference book?). Such decisions are also partly decided by the budget and how this is allocated. The physical durability and quality, including packaging, presentation, and cost are all important elements to be considered. These encompass the quality of illustrations, typography, layout and inclusion of maps and diagrams. These physical qualities include the quality of the footnotes, references, bibliography and the sequences and clearness of all the pagination. Other general criteria relate to existing stock, actual and potential growth areas in different subjects and school policy on the provision of text books and multiple copies (again related to teaching styles). The availability and quantity of items in satellite and departmental resource centres is also important. The ease with which other supplementary materials can be borrowed is also a help in deciding whether to buy or borrow, and in what quantities. What is available in local special collections may also be relevant, such as careers information and material, including information on local industry, and official publications. Cost and availability may be the criteria to be used here.

Many of the reviewing journals are also helpful in outlining criteria which they have used, but these journals tend to be used by librarians. This illustrates the need for a constant information flow from the library to teachers on new materials, so that they can help in the process of selection and apply meaningful criteria to items which they feel are of value to the library. Deciding in turn which journals to purchase depends also on the budget, how easily available they are elsewhere and whether any co-operative circulation scheme is in operation.

The defining and application of criteria are important, but are not activities which are an end in themselves. In the final analysis the interpretation of materials at a very personal level is the crucial moment, and this cannot be pre-determined. Many other factors are involved, including previous knowledge, expectations, personality and a host of unknown factors which each learner brings to each his or her unique situation when he or she uses materials.

The selection of materials of course involves stock rejection and stock evaluation, so that items already available also fulfil established criteria.

Print based materials — (selection criteria)

The physical (e.g. production) criteria to be applied here are familiar, including physical production (quality), date of publication, and the known characteristics of the publishing house. The inclusion of a contents list, good index, bibliography and biographical note on the author are known factors, as are good clear illustrations (at the right level), clear pagination, and clear chapter headings.

Much more difficult to assess are intellectual criteria, including the assessment of materials in relation to bias, usually relating to racial, sexual and political bias, but also including bias concerned with class, culture, status, and other more subtle forms, which are part of the current social and educational context. Some are blatantly overt, others covert, but careful selection processes need to be used by librarians. As in so many other areas, this may well involve some in-service training, although attitudes are incredibly difficult to change merely through using standard training techniques. The intellectual quality of visual illustrations, in relation to distortion, bias and presentation, in a direct or indirect politically or socially slanted context must also be considered. However, some very broad guidelines can be detected, and there is a considerable literature on the subject. The reviewing journals are becoming increasingly helpful in adding to the information available. This is particularly important when it is not possible to handle all potential purchases. Racial bias is one of the most important elements to be considered, as cultural differences must be recognised and the requirements of minority groups met. Materials in themselves cannot change attitudes, but they can contribute towards change. By applying reasoned criteria, some of the antisocial effects of biased material can be prevented. It is important to be aware of tokenism (the stereo-typed inclusion of minority groups), the reinforcing of existing prejudiced attitudes and the stereotyping of sexual, social or ethnic groups. Facts must be accurate, completely up to date, particularly in the political areas, and not presented in any slanted way. This must also be looked for in illustrations, as they too can reinforce existing prejudices. Librarians have a clear role to play here in helping to provide materials which support the emotional security of pupils, through providing materials which place cultural and other achievements in context, and also by providing materials for English as a second language course, in addition to mother tongue materials. There are problems in the provision of such materials, both in the availability of the books and materials produced commercially, and in the difficulty of tracing and ordering those published outside the UK. Bibliographical control is improving and many booksellers in other countries are becoming willing to accept 'blanket' orders from UK librarians.

Sexual bias is important also, and similar issues of distortion, prejudice and tokenism appear. Characterisation, language and illustrations are all used, or not used, to support bias in this area. Political bias is to some extent inherent in all materials as the views of the producers and writers are covertly or overtly presented. Bias of this nature is illustrated in the use of newspaper headlines and television news coverage, as well as in direct published formats. The librarian has a delicate role to play here, avoiding the pitfalls of representing one shade of opinion and neglecting others, or of supporting personal opinions, of whatever political shade. It is important to represent a reasonable range of opinion in resources provided which are supporting the curriculum, while at the same time encouraging a degree of political awareness. The same criteria apply to journals selected for the library, and these too should support the curriculum and the educational and personal needs of staff and pupils. Some represent the views of various social and minority groups, with a wide range of political opinion also, but their relevance to the curriculum and their valid, or otherwise, presentation of facts must be considered. Journals provide one source of 'instant information', in that they provide up-to-date material not yet published in book form, and purchase depends on the ways in which they can support project work, and inter-disciplinary work, cutting across traditional boundaries. They too can contribute to staff professional development.

This whole area rests a great deal on the social and political awareness of the librarian, and the ability to react with both sensitivity and common sense when making decisions. There cannot be any hard and fast rules. Criteria which relate to the selection of non print items (format, not intellectual content, where the same problems arise as with printed material), and equipment, are to some extent more straightforward.

The library and the librarian have to help support school and college policies, which should be part of the local and national response to positive care and concern. This concern will be illustrated not only by library resources, but by curriculum content, teachers' knowledge and sympathy, their professional development and links which are fostered between the school and the community. Librarians can provide support and resources for all these activities, including in-service training, and so have an active, not a passive role to play. The librarians' own personal attitudes are also important and can contribute to and influence the attitudes of others in the school. As well as positive influences, those of hidden antagonisms and prejudices also have to be considered. By integrating the work of the library into both school and authority work, the librarian can help support school policies through providing resource materials and through in-service training activities for teachers. He or she can also liaise in a positive way with inspectors and advisers, with specialist subject panels and those involved in the production of support materials, so that resource influence and provision works right across a spectrum of activities. Links can also be formed with counselling and pastoral care groups, providing books and information, and the same links and information can be established with any local community groups. This may involve working with local schools and colleges as well as with ethnic groups. Co-operation with publishers, both national and local, can also be productive, as so many are unaware of the needs of the multi-cultural classroom. These can in turn help provide materials for exhibitions and displays, and help supplement other cultural displays.

Bias in materials generally is related to sex, religion, race and culture, and a positive role by the library can counteract these influences.

Information — a selective list of relevant groups, institutes and associations

Africa Centre
38 King Street
London WC2

Afro-Caribbean Educational
Resources Project
ILEA Centre for Learning Resources
275 Kennington Lane
London SE11

Anti-Apartheid Movement
89 Charlotte Street
London W1

ATCAL (Association for the Teaching
of Caribbean & African Literature)
c/o Margaret Butcher
c/o Commonwealth Institute
Kensington High Street
London W8

Campaign Against Racism in the
Media (CARM)
P.O. Box 50
London N1

Caribbean Communications Project
470 Harrow Road
London W9

Caribbean Cultural Centre
Karnak House
300 Westbourne Park Road
London W11

Centre for Language in Primary
Education (ILEA)
Ebury Teachers Centre
Sutherland Street
London SW1

Centre for Multi-Racial Education
165a Cromwell Road
Peterborough PE1 P2EL

Centre for Urban Educational Studies
(ILEA)
Robert Montefiore School
Underwood Road
Whitechapel
London E1 5AD

Centre for World Development
Education
128 Buckingham Palace Road
London SW1

Childrens Rights Workshop
73 Balfour Street
London SE17

Commission for Racial Equality
Elliot House
10-12 Allington Street
London SW1E 5EH

Commonwealth Institute
Kensington High Street
London W8

Equal Opportunities Commission
Overseas House
Quay Street
Manchester

Institute of Race Relations
247 Pentonville Road
London N1

NAME (National Association for
Multiracial Education)
48 Lewisham High Street
London SE13

National Association of Afro-
Caribbean Libraries
c/o Hornsey Library
Haringay Park
London N8

National Council for Civil Liberties
186 Kings Cross Road
London WC1

University of London
School of Oriental & Asian Studies
(SOAS)
Extramural Dept
Malet Street
London WC1

Runnymede Trust
62 Chandos Place
London WC2

Writers and Readers Cooperative
Camden High Street
London NW1

● Journals — a selective list

Aslib Book News
Aslib
3 Belgrave Square
London SW1X 8PL

Dragons Teeth
National Committee Against Racism
in Childrens Books
46 High Street
Southall, Middlesex

Books for Keeps
School Bookshop Association
National Book League
Book House
45 East Hill
Wandsworth
London SW18

Education Journal
Commission for Racial Equality
Elliot House
10-12 Allington Street
London SW1E 5EH

Books for your Children
Ann Ward
90 Gillhurst Road
Harborne
Birmingham 17

English Centre Magazine
Ebury Teachers Centre (ILEA)
Sutherland Street
London SW1

British Book News
British Council
65 Davies Street
London W1V 2AA

Ethnic and Racial Studies
Routledge and Kegan Paul
Boundary House
New Town Road
Henley on Thames

Childrens Book Bulletin
Childrens Rights Workshop
4 Aldebert Terrace
London SW1

Grass Roots
61 Golbourne Road
Westbourne Park
London W10

Interracial Books for Children Bulletin
Council on Interracial Books for
Children
1841 Broadway
New York, N.Y. 10023
USA

Issues in Race & Education
45 Anson Road
London N7 0AR

Minority Rights Groups Reports
36 Craven Street
London WC2

NAME Journal
National Association for Multiracial
Education
23 Doles Lane
Findern
Derby DE6 6AX

New Internationalist
62A High Street
Wallingford
Oxon

Oxfam News
Oxfam Education Department
274 Banbury Road
Oxford OXL 7DX

Race and Class
Institute of Race Relations
247 Pentonville Road
London N1

Race Today
74 Shakespeare Road
London SE24

School Book Review
Europa Publications Limited
18 Bedford Square
London WC1B 3JN

Times Educational Supplement
P.O. Box 7
200 Grays Inn Road
London WC1X 8EZ

Times Literary Supplement
P.O. Box 7
200 Grays Inn Road
London WC1X 8EZ

● **References — a selective list of relevant books, reports and articles**

Commission for Racial Equality. *Racialism and sexism in books — a checklist.* (Reprinted from *Education and Community Relations)* London, Commission for Racial Equality, 1975.

Craft, M. (ed.) *Teaching the multi-cultural society: the task for teacher education.* Lewes, Falmer Press, 1981.

Dixon, R. *Catching them young. 1: sex, race and class in children's fiction.* London, Pluto Press, 1977.

Education and the urban environment, units 11-13. *Race, children and cities.* Milton Keynes, Open University, 1979. (Course E361).

Elkin, J. *(comp.) Multi-racial books for the classroom: a select list of children's books,* 3rd rev. ed. London, Library Association Youth Libraries Group, 1980.

Elliott, P. *Library needs of children attending mother-tongue schools in London.* London, Polytechnic of North London, 1981. (School of Librarianship Research Report No. 6).

Hartman, P. and Husband, C. *Racism and the mass media.* London, Davis Poynter, 1974.

Inner London Education Authority. *Education in a multi-ethnic society: an aide memoire for the Inspectorate.* London, ILEA, 1981.

In-service teacher education in a multi-racial society. Windsor, NFER, CED, ICME and University of Keele.

Interim report of the Rampton (Swann) Committee of Enquiry into the Achievement of ethnic minority children. London, HMSO, 1981.

Klein, G. 'Multicultural materials' in *Times Educational Supplement,* London, 20 November 1981.

Klein, G. *Resources for multicultural education: an introduction.* York, Longmans, 1982.

Little, A. and Willey, R. *Multi-ethnic education: the way forward.* London, Schools Council, 1981.

Lynch, J. *Teaching in the multi-cultural school.* London, Ward Lock Educational, 1981.

National Book League. *Books for the multi-cultural classroom.* London, NBL, 1971.

National Union of Teachers. *All our children.* London, NUT, 1978.

Policy Studies Institute. *Policy and practice in the multi-racial city: a report.* London, PSI, 1981.

Policy Studies Institute. *Social service provision in multi-racial areas: a research paper.* London, PSI, 1981.

Schools Council. *Multicultural education: the way forward.* London, Schools Council, 1981.

Stinton, J. (ed.) *Racism and sexism in children's books.* London, Writers and Readers Cooperative, 1979.

Troyna, B. *Public awareness and the media.* London, Commission for Racial Equality, 1981.

Vincent, K. *A survey of the methods by which teachers select books.* Sheffield, CRUS, 1980. (CRUS occasional paper no. 3). (British Library R & D Report No. 5549).

Whittaker, K. *Systematic evaluation: methods and sources for evaluating books.* London, Bingley, 1982.

Willey, R. *Teaching in multi-cultural Britain.* London, Schools Council, 1982.

Zimet, S.G. *Print and prejudice.* London, Hodder & Stoughton, 1976.

Planning pointers

- Determine authority policies.

- Establish, define and apply criteria, relating to both the intellectual and physical characteristics of new materials.

- Make sure that these are compatible with and acceptable within school policy.

- Relate materials to curriculum content and innovation.

- Relate materials to teaching and learning styles.

- Select in relation to existing stock, as well as long term plans for stock control.

- Be aware of political, sexual and racial bias. Be aware of personal bias.

- Constantly evaluate and weed stock in co-operation with members of the teaching staff, and any specialist staff.

- Utilise all local specialised agencies and experts.

- Be informed on national developments.

This broad group of materials can be broken down into smaller groupings or clusters, and while some general criteria apply to all of them, some are concerned with specific physical formats only. Within this broad spectrum it is possible to isolate groups which include three dimensional objects, miscellaneous packs and kits, still visuals, including microforms, moving visuals, and aural materials. All are information carriers for the purposes of bibliographical organisation, but many need special treatment for access and storage.

It is difficult to preview these materials, partly because of the problems of national bibliographic control, partly owing to a lack of good reviews, and partly owing to the mechanical problems involved in purchasing. Because of these problems once an item is in stock it has to be of value, as replacing it can take time. Relationships with the curriculum are crucial, as is use of resource materials both centrally and departmentally. Patterns of resource use need to be considered. Physical production and quality are important criteria, as some items are expensively packaged and the contents do not necessarily relate to the cost. Quality includes good graphics, visuals, sound and packaging. The organisation of the information, as part of the physical production, corresponds to the contents lists, chapter headings and references in a book. Details include the need for clear numbering of sequences, explicit numbered frames (if appropriate) and teachers' notes. The pacing of information also has to fit the physical format chosen, and this in turn has to relate to the subject. For example, processes can be more effectively illustrated through film or video than through print. The format also can helpfully relate to the intended age level — simpler productions are easier for younger pupils to handle. The use of recorded materials is an important area to consider, as these can be biased or distorted, but carry with them an air of authority. Format also impinges on the criteria for use, as materials for individual work are not necessarily suitable for large group or class work. The uses of data bases (Dialogue, Blaise etc.) are a case in point. The equipment available (and its compatibility) if there is little money to purchase new items, will also help decide if resources are to be bought. Linked with this is the availability and use of spaces, power points and blackout in relation to the intended use of items — both costs and use may be the criteria here. Storage and safety also need to be considered.

Other criteria relate to the effectiveness of the media in relation to specific learning tasks and the anticipated outcomes of these tasks. So in the selection process it is important to know for whom the resource is intended, if it is to be used as a teaching or learning instrument (e.g. the type of task) and the characteristics of the media involved. Its value as an information carrier may also be very relevant, as for example in the case of video, which has dense information capacity, is simple to use, easy to organise, and can deal with graphic, alphanumeric and pictorial forms of information. This is enhanced through the use of video interface with computers (VIC). Microforms are important carriers of information — a high density information carrier which is easy both to use and to organise. These attributes may be as important or more important than the physical qualities of the item. Resources have different characteristics in presenting information, and hence different uses, stemming from the first planning stages. Some media present information at a general level, while others present it more positively — for example, slides positively convey information in the form of words, diagrams, pictures, graphics and patterns. Again there is considerable literature on the subject, and although the boundaries may still be blurred it will become an increasingly important area as students expect to learn in relation to their own personal needs and expectations.

Non-print materials — software packages

The basic selection criteria for the acquisition of these materials follow the same general principles of their relationship to curriculum content and organisation, availability of hardware, staffing availability and levels, and local policies, among others. The cost of programmes, their scope, flexibility in the teaching learning situation, the extent to which they have been tested and used elsewhere in an educational context, and their compatibility with existing and planned developments are all important aspects to consider before purchase. The existence of any local expertise and advice both in the planning of and exchange of expertise and packages, is also important, as is extent of authority support in the in-service training area. The need both to provide for local conditions and at the same time to aim at national standardisation to improve access is a dilemma which is helped through adequate authority support.

● Information — a selective list of relevant groups, institutes and associations

Arlis
Secretary — Graham Bullock
Hull College of Higher Education
Queens Gardens
Hull HU1 3DH

Aslib
Audio Visual Group
Aslib
3 Belgrave Square
London SW1X 8PL

British Film Institute
127-133 Charing Cross Road
London WC2H 0EA

British Industrial and Scientific Film
Association
26 D'Arblay Street
London W1V 6AA

British Universities Film Council
81 Dean Street
London W1V 6AA

Educational Television Association
86 Micklegate
York YO1 1JL

Library Association Audiovisual
Group
Library Association
7 Ridgmount Street
London WC1E 7AE

Microfilm Association of Great
Britain
Longman Group Ltd
6th Floor
Westgate House
The High
Harlow, Essex

National Sound Archive (BIRS)
29 Exhibition Road
London SW7

Society for Education in Film and
Television
20 Old Compton Street
London W1

Society of Picture Libraries and
Agencies
31 Haddon Court
Milton Road
Harpenden
Herts

● Journals — a selective list

Arts Libraries Society Newsheet
G. Bullock
Arlis Secretary
Hull College of Higher Education
Queens Gardens
Hull HU1 3DH

Audio Visual
P.O. Box 109
McLaren House
Scarbrook Road
Croydon
Surrey CR9 1QH

Audiovisual Librarian
Audiovisual Groups of Aslib and the
Library Association
Library Association Publishing
7 Ridgmount Street
London WC1E 7AE

Cassette Scrutiny
School of Library & Information
Science
Ealing College of Higher Education
St. Mary's Road
Ealing
London W5 5RF

CET News
Council for Educational Technology
3 Devonshire Street
London W1N 2BA

Infuse
British Library Information Officer for
User Education
Loughborough University of
Technology
Loughborough
Leics. LE11 3TU

*Journal of Educational Television and
Other Media*
Educational Television Association
7 Micklegate
York YO1 1JZ

Material Matters
Hertfordshire County Library
Services
County Hall
Hertford SG13 8AJ

School Library Media Quarterly
American Association of School
Librarians
50 East Huron Street
Chicago
Illinois IL60 611
USA

Screen Digest
Screen Digest Ltd
37 Gower Street
London WC1E 6HH

Screen Education
(SEFT)
20 Old Compton Street
London W1

Times Educational Supplement
P.O. Box 7
200 Grays Inn Road
London WC1X 8EZ

Video
Link House Magazines
Croydon
Surrey

Videogram
Nord Media Ltd
37 New Bond Street
London W1

Videoinfo
Microinfo Ltd
P.O. Box 3
Alton
Hants GU34 2PG

● **References — a selective list of relevant books, reports and articles**

Berger, J. *Ways of seeing.* Harmondsworth, Penguin, 1972.
Bloom, B.S. *Taxonomy of educational objectives.* New York, McKay, 1956.

Briggs, L.J. (ed.) *Instructional Design: Principles and applications.* Englewood Cliffs, N.J., Educational Technology Publications, 1977.

British Film Institute. *Reading pictures.* London, Academic Press, 1978.

Cabeceiras, J. *The multimedia library.* London, Academic Press, 1978.

Curran, J. et al. *Mass communication and society.* London, Arnold, 1977.

Fiske, J. and Hartley, J. *Reading the television.* London, Methuen, 1978.

Gagne, R.M. *Conditions of learning.* 3rd ed. New York, Holt Rinehart & Winston, 1977.

Gagne, R.M. and Briggs, L.J. *Principles of instructional design.* New York, Holt Rinehart & Winston, 1977.

Greenhalgh, M. *Audio cassettes: a guide to selection and management.* Oxford, School Library Association, 1982.

Masterman, L. *Teaching about television.* London, Macmillan, 1980.

Salomon, G. and Clark, R.E. 'Re-examining the methodology of research on media and technology in education' in *Review of Educational Research,* 1977 (47) (1) pp. 99-120.

Williams, B. and Fothergill, R. *Microforms in Education.* London, CET, 1977 (Working Paper 13).

Planning pointers

- Determine authority policies.

- Establish, define and apply criteria relating to both intellectual and physical factors of materials.

- Make sure that these are compatible with and acceptable as part of school policy.

- Relate materials to teaching and learning styles.

- Be informed about physical criteria. Relate these to resources policies (organisation and control of materials).

- Be aware of the relationship of the media selected to the intended teaching or learning task.

- Co-operate in any local schemes which are concerned with current developments, such as the exchange of software packages.

Criteria for the selection of equipment relate to systems and to equipment. Systems, a term used here to include word processors, on-line retrieval systems, teletext systems and others, are generally speaking installed as a result of local authority decisions at a fairly high level, or possibly as a result of research funding. It is important to distinguish between criteria relating to such major systems and those relating to equipment which will be used in conjunction with learning resource materials (software) and for in-house or local production of materials. Many criteria follow constraints already in operation, at a variety of levels, and for many reasons, particularly those of economics and cost. Questions have to be asked about costs, time, space, staff and future policies. Because of these inherent constraints involved in the purchase of equipment it is advisable to carry out a relatively detailed survey before any decisions are made, so that planning questions help both to provide the answers to questions and to provide relevant criteria.

At the technical level it is important to consider what is required from any item of equipment, which has in itself clearly defined limits of use. Installation and running costs, the variety of models available, comparability studies, specifications available, and the availability of demonstrations (equivalent to previewing) and 'trial runs' should be considered. Durability (possibly portability) and the 'user friendly' aspects need to be considered, plus any servicing or maintenance problems and their costs. This also includes any extra technical or maintenance staffing costs. The user specifications issued by the CET (USPECS) are very helpful.

The design and technical competence of the machine, and its relationship to any standardisation policy is also important. Security, safety, power points, space and ergonomics all relate to criteria at the technical level.

Other aspects of technical details include the availability and amount of software (in the widest sense), such as commercially available materials, locally produced items, and the possibilities and cost of producing in-house software. If materials have to be produced in-house, then the costs of extra staffing at several levels would also have to be considered. The organisation and maintenance problems of any software also have to be considered. Access to a printer and access to hard copy (in the case of data bases) are also important.

At the school or college level another series of questions relates to somewhat broader issues. These include the nature of equipment already in stock, its efficiency and patterns of use (by whom and when). Compatibility with existing equipment is important, both at the school and the local level (for any co-operative schemes to work). The ease of operation and quality of results must be considered. The problem of the design of supporting software at the school level is crucial, as this must support the school curricular objectives and so the two must match. The school or college may or may not have a developmental policy, and so the way in which change is managed is another criterion. Part of such a policy is an establishment structure, or structures, at either formal or informal level for assessing and reviewing new developments. The involvement of key people within the school is important, plus their positions in the hierarchy and in any developmental committees. The availability, organisation and access to planned and existing spaces are criteria to be considered.

At the local and national level policies can also determine criteria. These may or may not exist in relation to particular groups or items of equipment but, if they do exist, they must be considered and can relate to purchasing policies and to maintenance. These problems are also linked to the extent and availability of both school and authority in-service training schemes, at technician, teacher and policy member levels. These will also partly dictate if any networks exist locally and how well used they are. The current climate also has an effect on decisions, as more changes take place at times of economic prosperity.

If, however, there are few alternatives, either in terms of systems, equipment, software or strategies, then decisions may be made as a result of negative criteria.

● Information — a selective list of relevant groups, institutes and associations

Association for Educational and
Training Technology
BLAT Centre
BMA House
Tavistock Square
London WC1H 9JP

British Educational Equipment
Association
10 Gunthorpe Street
London E1

Council for Educational Technology
(USPECS)
3 Devonshire Street
London W1N 2BA

Library Association
Working Party on New Technology
7 Ridgmount Street
London WC1E 7AE

National Foundation for Visual Aids
National Audio Visual Aids Centre
Paxton Place
Gipsy Road
London SE27 9SR

● Journals — a selective list

Audio Visual
P.O. Box 109
MacLaren House
Scarbrook Road
Croydon
Surrey CR9 1QH

Audiovisual Librarian
Audiovisual Groups of Aslib and the
Library Association
Library Association Publishing
7 Ridgmount Street
London WC1E 7AH

CET News
Council for Educational Technology
3 Devonshire Street
London W1N 2BA

Education Equipment
Benn Publications Ltd
Sovereign Way
Tonbridge
Kent TN9 1YZ

Educational Technology
Educational Technology Publications
Inc
140 Sylvan Avenue
Englewood Cliffs, NJ 07632
USA

*Programmed Learning & Educational
Technology*
Association for Educational and
Training Technology
Kogan Page
120 Pentonville Road
London N1

Screen Digest
Screen Digest Ltd
37 Gower Street
London WC1E 6HH

Video
Link House Magazines
Croydon
Surrey

Videogram
Nord Media Ltd
37 New Bond Street
London W1

● **References — a selective list of relevant books, reports and articles**

Audio Visual Handbook. London, Kogan Page, 1982.

Council for Educational Technology. *Focus on safety: a guide to the safe handling and operation of audiovisual equipment.* London, CET, 1979 (USPEC 26).

Council for Educational Technology. *Learning resources in colleges: their organisation and management.* London, CET, 1981.

Council for Educational Technology. *Audio visual resources in secondary schools: their organisation and management.* London, CET, 1980.

International Yearbook of Educational and Instructional Technology, 1980/81. Kogan Page, 1980.

Page, G.T. and Whitlock, Q. (eds) *Aspects of educational technology XIII: 'Educational technology twenty years on'* Kogan Page, 1979. (Proceedings of the 1979 APLET Conference).

Planning pointers

- Find out authority policies on equipment purchase and use.

- Find out school policies on equipment purchase and use.

- Establish and define criteria which relate to both large scale systems and to individual items of proposed equipment.

- Find out level and extent of in-service training support.

- Check extent of technical maintenance, plus costs.

- Keep up to date with new developments and be aware of their educational potential. Attend relevant courses which relate hardware to curriculum development.

- Relate all new purchases to available software.

Many of the general principles of the application of criteria apply to the field of microcomputers. Principles do not change even if the items to which they are being applied change. It may be helpful to consider some general points, as computers form part of a rapidly evolving area.

They are one more resource in the educational armoury, and can be used and integrated into all areas of the curriculum, from the management of information (statistics, pupil numbers etc.), and the provision of library and other 'housekeeping' programmes to relate to the needs of individual schools, to individual collections supporting the curriculum. They can also provide individual help and programmes for individual students. Again, there is a need for a co-ordinated policy at local and national levels, particularly important in the provision of software, where the situation now closely resembles the early days of tape slide productions and videotapes. Research is also contributing to this area and helping establish criteria for selection and use.

The general criteria follow the same principles as those used in the selection of any learning resources materials. They include ways in which the school or college wants to be involved in computing technology, either at an administrative level or at a curricular level in individual teaching and learning experiences.

The selection and purchase of software is identical to the processes used in the selection of both print and non print materials, as computer programmes are merely another form of information carrier. Analysing costs and objectives is crucial. Purposes, needs, availability, compatibility, and policies are all relevant. Software must match the educational objectives of the school or college, and programmes must relate to any learning requirements. They must also be structured in a meaningful way, and it must be possible to give feedback to the learner, and to provide further support if necessary. The storage and handling of programmes must also be considered. Programmes must include clear instructions on use and on the reaction expected from the user. Screen presentation, and the ways in which programmes can be used in conjunction with other programmes, are also important. As yet the software has not caught up with the hardware, and the rigorous application of both establishment and personal criteria is important as otherwise the pupil will receive little real benefit. Computer assisted learning, computer managed learning, computer assisted instruction and telesoftware systems are all contributing to open learning situations, and as the pupil or student can increasingly move at his or her own pace, can provide more initiatives in the ways in which he or she wants to learn. The teacher also has more freedom in designing the curriculum. They are part of an increasingly interactive teaching and learning process.

The selection and purchase of hardware relates to local and national policies as well as costs. Portability may be important and durability again an important criteria, as smaller machines can get a considerable amount of use. Good (and easily available) local servicing facilities are important in making decisions. (These can be either local authority or commercial servicing agencies but their availability is crucial. Even the most well organised schools will not always be able to remedy faults). The availability of hard copy services must be considered, together with the availability of good explanatory material in addition to worksheets, guides and users' manuals. In-service training facilities, either provided locally or through funds provided for access to national training facilities, are also important. Such training in the use of hardware must of course be linked to the production and use of software. Maintenance funding must be available.

At present there are numerous sources of information, advice and expertise at all levels, plus a fast growing literature. There is also a multiplicity of users' groups, formal and informal, and librarians could and should be involved in these. Computers can be used as managers (CML), instructors (CAL, CAI, CAT), administrators, and research aids, and each group of users has its own group literature field.

This new dimension in the resource field has enormous potential and many advantages. Some of these are relatively easy to distinguish. The computer can be paced to suit the individual learner, and so can encourage the learner to develop within the limits of his or her styles and needs. Individual students thus have some control over the learning process. A computer programme is patient, and can operate independently of a teacher, and also can reward through instant feedback (the answers can be seen). Programmes can be used for simulation exercises, particularly useful in areas where experiments would be very expensive, or those that involve a wide range of personnel and resources, such as pollution, medicine and traffic control. Revision exercises, problem solving exercises, decision making exercises and open ended discussions are all possible. This width of availability can help to broaden the curriculum, enhance teaching standards and also expand the amount of information available, not only through access to programmes, but also through access to other data bases. Their interactive use, as with the Open University system (Cyclops) and the adaptation of Prestel (Optel) also has tremendous potential. The linking of videodiscs with computers has enormous potential as a teaching and learning tool, as a vast amount of information (stored in the disc) can be used through an interface with a microcomputer, thus giving students access to the advantages of both systems, and producing an interactive but individualised teaching and learning situation.

Problems relate to the defining of realistic criteria, teacher and pupil reactions, and to bibliographic control and organisation of software. It is also important to assess developments and materials in relation to systems and materials which may already be available at less cost. Expense, compatibility of both hardware and software, copyright teething troubles which normally accompany innovation, and the need for standardisation are all current problems. Effective evaluation and monitoring of pupils' progress may present difficulties, which in turn form part of the problem of training and re-training staff in conjunction with existing patterns and needs.

Information — a selective list of relevant groups, institutes and associations

Advisory Unit for Computer Based
Education
(AUCBE)
Endymion Road
Hatfield
Herts

Aslib
3 Belgrave Square
London SW1X 8PL

British Library Research &
Development Department
2 Sheraton Street
London W1V 4BH

British Videogram Association
10 Maddox Street
London W1R 9N

CEDAR Project (Computers in
Education as a Resource)
Information Officer
Imperial College Computer Centre
Exhibition Road
London SW7 2BX

Council for Educational Technology
3 Devonshire Street
London W1N 2BA

Microcomputers in Primary
Education
c/o Upwood School
Upwood
Huntingdon
Cambs, PE17 1QA

Microelectronics Education Project
(Director — R. Fothergill)
Cheviot House
Coach Lane Campus
Newcastle-upon-Tyne
NE7 7XA

National Computing Centre
Oxford Road
Manchester M1 7ED

RML Users Group
(Research Machines Ltd)
c/o Peter South
Educational Computing Centre
Chelsea College
552 Kings Road
London SW10

Journals — a selective list

Appropriate Technology
Intermediate Technology
Publications Ltd
9 King Street
London WC2E 8HN

*British Journal of Educational
Technology*
Council for Educational Technology
3 Devonshire Street
London W1N 2BA

101

CAL News
Council for Educational Technology
3 Devonshire Street
London W1N 2BA

Computers and Education
Pergamon Press
Headington Hill Hall
Oxford OX3 0BW

Educational Research
National Foundation for Educational
Research
2 Oxford Road East
Windsor
Berks

● **References — a selective list of relevant books, reports and articles**

The CAL Bibliography. (Microfiche). CEDAR Project. Imperial College Computer Centre, Exhibition Road, London SW7 2BX.

The CAL Package Index. (Microfiche). CEDAR Project. Imperial College Computer Centre, Exhibition Road, London SW7 2BX.

Fielden, J. and Pearson, P.K. *The cost of learning with computers.* London, CET, 1978.

Hooper, R. and Toye, I. (eds) *Computer assisted learning in the United Kingdom — some case studies.* London, CET, 1975.

Horner, G. and Teskey, F. J. 'Microcomputers and the school library' in *School Librarian, 27* (4) December 1979, pp 339-40.

Library Association. School Libraries Group. *The microelectronics revolution and its implication for the school library.* London, School Libraries Group, 1982.

Payne, T. 'Computerised information in secondary schools: organic growth and institutional influence' in *The nationwide provision and use of information.* Aslib/IIS/CA joint conference, Sheffield, September 1980, Proceedings. London, LA, 1981, pp 282-91.

Planning pointers — general

● Distinguish between long and short term plans. Also distinguish between print and non print items and equipment.

● Formulate library plans for their provision in relation to schools and college plans.

● Work out a series of planning questions so that policies can logically follow these.

● Learning resources (and equipment) must support the educational and social life of the school or college, so co-operate and liaise as much as possible over the definition and application of criteria.

● Have a library statement or statements giving criteria for selection which clearly reflects these school views. Use existing procedures (committees etc.) to help in selecting materials. If these do not exist try and establish them; initiate new ideas.

● Utilise all support available over selecting resources which can support a rapidly changing society.

● Utilise reviews and specialist collections and keep up to date on educational theories and changes in practice.

● Be prepared and informed at personal level so that the library takes an active not a passive role in the selection of learning resources. Keep up to date with technical developments.

● Beware of creating bandwagons flying the new technology flag.

Planning pointers

- Establish, define and apply criteria relating to the purchase and use of microcomputers for library resource centre use.

- Define and apply criteria relating to hardware and software.

- Try to avoid purchasing software which does not have a well defined and established market.

- Ensure that there is adequate support, including documentation, instruction and manuals.

- Relate the criteria for the selection of printed and other materials to the selection of software, including bias, credibility, stated objectives, suitability, etc.

- Find out the extent and level of in-service training support.

- Join any relevant local groups or networks.

- Keep up to date with new developments in educational contexts and librarianship contexts.

Acquisition

This whole area is an integral part of the educational scene. Books and materials are 'apparent' resources which are prone to cuts in unfavourable economic times, although they are used as a yardstick to measure success and good provision on a national level. They belong both to a very traditional organisational world and a very rapidly changing technological one. As the area is well documented, relevant information will not be reproduced here, but can be obtained from the sources quoted.

The actual acquisition of books and other materials, once they have been selected, thus forms part of the complicated structure of the British publishing and bookselling trade. This includes the intricacies of Resale Price Maintenance and the Net Book Agreement, full details of which can be obtained from the Booksellers and Publishers Associations. The Library Licence forms a part of these conditions, as it allows libraries to purchase net books at a discount.

As far as school and college librarians are concerned, the acquisition of books is bound up with the need for both previewing and processing services, the ways in which both teachers and librarians are informed of new publications, the ways in which they select materials, and the reasons (or lack of them) for these decisions. These decisions form part of the curricular constraints (text books and related materials have to be ordered), the professional needs of teachers, and the influence of a professional librarian within a school who has knowledge of and access to information sources. The recent CRUS survey quoted in the bibliography, illustrates the difficulties teachers have in obtaining information on new materials and making informed decisions on purchases.

The school librarian has a very active role to play here, in the collection of information in print and non print format, distribution of information to teachers, a policy of stock selection and retrieval which relates to the school curricula, and making sure that all support services from the authority are utilised. Good links with local and specialist booksellers are important and book clubs and bookshops located in the library are valuable. Access to on-line data bases should make it easier for librarians to provide a good information service, and there is now potential for on line ordering systems to be developed. The development of electronic publishing will also be an important aspect of relating supply and demand to information.

The development of the use of the new technology will help both to prevent the costly involvement of librarians in tasks which are not professional, and to provide an improved information and delivery service and a much more realistic relationship between the demands of the changing curriculum and the availability of materials. Librarians have to utilise these developments in their planning, both in the structure and organisation of staff, and in the planning of services.

● **Information — a selective list of relevant groups, institutes and associations**

Booksellers Association
154 Buckingham Palace Road
London SW1

Chartered Institute of Public Finance
and Accountancy
1 Buckingham Place
London SW1E 6HS

Colleges of Further and Higher
Education Group
Library Association
7 Ridgmount Street
London WC1E 7AE

Educational Publishers Council
Publishers Association
19 Bedford Square
London WC1B 3JE

National Book League
Book House
45 East Hill
London SW18 2HZ

Publishers Association
19 Bedford Square
London WC1B 3JE

School Bookshop Association
1 Effingham Road
London SW18 2HZ

School Libraries Group
Library Assocation
7 Ridgmount Street
London WC1E 7AE

Youth Libraries Group
Library Association
7 Ridgmount Street
London WC1E 7AE

● **Journals — a selective list**

Bookseller
J. Whitaker & Sons Ltd
12 Dyott Street
London WC1

British National Bibliography
British Library Bibliographical
Services Division
2 Sheraton Street
London W1V 4BH

● **References — a selective list of relevant books, reports and articles**

Committee of Enquiry into the supply of books to schools and colleges. (Report of the Lady David Committee). London, Educational Publishers Council, 1981.

National Book League. *Books for schools: report of the National Book League Working Party.* London, NBL, 1979.

Use of journal subscription agents. Loughborough, CLAIM, 1981 (management check list no. 1).

Vincent, K. *A survey of the methods by which teachers select books.* Sheffield, CRUS, 1980 (Crus occasional papers 3).

Planning pointers

- Try and tailor services to fit the needs of the curriculum and of the community.

- Find out what services are available (bookshops, authority supply agencies or educational contractors) and the extent of these services in the authority.

- Check on the availability of information services, selection and previewing services, processing services (and their flexibility) plus costs. These can relate to local services (as above) or national services.

- Determine the financial procedures for ordering materials. Check on flexibility needed when ordering 'minority' materials produced by small organisations, for example.

- Determine what committee procedures are involved, and participate if possible.

- Maintain an efficient information service on new materials.

- Keep up to date with technological developments such as document delivery services and 'on-demand' publishing developments.

Planning: access, organisation of space and storage
(new and existing areas, single site and multi-site)

The planning and use of the conversion of existing spaces or the planning of new spaces clearly relates to the amount of support, advice, organisational constraints, and direct control from the local authority as well as from the establishment, in addition to constraints imposed by finance, safety regulations, legal requirements, and architectural constraints. Others will be imposed by the existing users of spaces, linked both to historical use in relation to teaching and learning activities, to any library tradition, and to the power base within the school/college. Empire building equates with space! Figures which relate to basic national standards, such as office accommodation, study areas and storage areas as well as minimum stock figures, are contained in *Library resource provision in schools: guidelines and recommendations*, published by the Library Association. The Association has also published standards for colleges, as have Natfhe, Cofhe and the DES.

The basic concepts relate to all establishments, regardless of size, and involve a systematic approach to the problem. Any space must relate to others, in both its planning and its use. The first planning point is deciding if the space is to be open or closed access. Decisions on the organisation and use of spaces can be made as a result of asking a series of planning questions, which help to analyse the situation, rather than merely acquire space. These may include the question of the total current space allocated for library resource use, and what could be changed to provide more without re-building?

How much original or extra space is needed? What long term plans are in the pipeline (e.g. those involving teaching and learning activities) which will affect the use of space? What are the current constraints? Does the present space work — i.e. can planned activities take place easily and comfortably? What peripheral or satellite resource centres are already being used or are in the planning stages? The users also should be consulted over their perception of the functions of the library resource centre, and the ways in which they see their relationship both with it and with other users. If necessary, the physical site should be viewed. An interim report with as many details as possible should then be written. If this is for a new space, as many data as possible should be included for planning purposes.

The next stage should involve analysing the activities which will take place within the library resource centre, as these will help to decide the form which the physical area will have, and the form then determines the function of the centre. Functions are then confirmed by the original policy statement and objectives. These activities can cover a wide range and so initially is is necessary to analyse and group them, so that spaces can be planned. Any specific materials or activities which require particular accommodation needs must be catered for plus the materials and equipment they involve. The majority of activities can be grouped either under formal teaching and learning activities (individual and group), the same activities at an informal level, casual activities, and administration. They range, for example, from individual pupil study activities using materials in all formats including on-line data bases, to group activities, which may include both staff and students. Teaching and research can also be carried out singly or in groups.

More casual activities include browsing, discussion, producing materials, story telling, presenting reports, using journals, illustrating the use of materials, and preparing models and displays. In addition to these operations the materials themselves need to be stored and/or displayed, in relation to their physical format, their use, and their requirement for any equipment. The planning and purchasing of equipment (hardware) needs to be considered as an integral part of all other activities and available resources. Note will have to be taken of health and safety regulations. Technical advice on various items of equipment can be obtained from the Council for Educational Technology, in the form of user specifications (USPECS). Authority advice and expertise will also be available. (Criteria for purchasing software and hardware are considered in earlier sections.) Materials include a variety of physical formats, ranging from microforms, videodiscs and on-line information, to reference materials and ephemera on current affairs. Some will require special storage systems and instruction, and help over their use while others can be stored on the open shelves, with any necessary equipment nearby. Other spaces, not suitable for individual study, may be available for storing little-used materials, and this should be planned in conjunction with any local schemes of subject specialisation or co-operative purchase.

The exploitation of materials at a more informal level, through displays, exhibitions, special collections, visiting speakers etc., also requires space and specialised storage. Useful links can be formed with any museum or similar service.

The production of materials can be done at a very simple level by pupils and staff, as mentioned earlier, including making overhead projector transparencies, audio tapes, slides and other projected and non projected materials. These will be made as part of the planned use of the library. The location and organisation of other production activities, such as library guides (video, tape-slide, print etc.), booklets, curriculum support materials for both teacher and pupil use, and any other in-house productions, will depend on other external factors. These will include the level of centralised support (plus time and costs), and the level of establishment support, in terms of staff, equipment and space. The planning of production areas has to take note of these constraints and existing services.

The administrative areas also have to be considered, again in relation to functions. Materials have to be borrowed and loaned, equipment serviced, borrowed or loaned, items ordered, processed and shelved and all other routine tasks carried out. The allocation of service areas to these activities will again depend on any central services, and on the individual school/ college needs. In addition to service areas, administrative professional and volunteer staff also need more private spaces in which to work, to relax, and to entertain visitors. They also need areas where they can talk privately to pupils. Informal pupil/student counselling is a delicate 'fringe' activity which needs space, but which must be recognised as an area where a member of the library staff can provide support but not expertise — he or she must channel any problems to the experts.

The planning of learning to learn activities, embracing user education activities, overlaps many of these other activities and cannot be looked at in isolation. The use of the library resource centre, in its widest sense, will depend on curriculum content and organisation, and so the planning of spaces will stem from this. There may be a need for areas for group discussion, for individual and planned project work based on effectively getting to grips with information, for formal seminar rooms, informal discussions areas, small scale production areas, or a combination of any of these.

The use of space then helps resolve decisions on ventilation, heating, lighting, flooring, power points, blackout facilities, service outlets including water, furniture, shelving, storage units, and the location and storage of equipment. Colour is also an important point which needs consideration. The extent of community involvement will also help resolve some details. This detail will of course vary enormously in differing establishments, and to a large extent depends on central and local circumstances. Such detail, even though involving considerable expense, should include the planning of furniture. This includes form, shape and colour, in relation to use, as well as durability and flexibility. The ease of cleaning furniture, and ways of storing tables and chairs are also important. Furniture such as carrels must also relate to standards of safety. The ways in which furniture can be placed within the space are also important and so traffic flow, grouping, single and group activities and control must all be considered. At all stages there is a need for co-operation during planning, but it becomes clear when expertise is needed over heating, lighting and other technical areas. There is always expertise available from the authority, correlating to its structure and organisation. It is also helpful to foster other local units, and tap other expertise in colleges, polytechnics, universities, schools and community centres. Some can and will provide direct advice

1 Table
1 back panel
2 end panels
1 electrical service unit

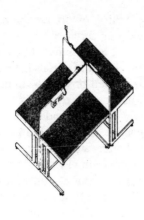

2 Tables
2 back panels
1 end panel
2 electrical service units
2 cable clips

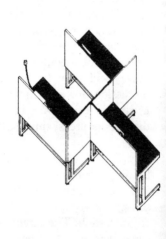

2 Tables
1 back panel
1 end panel
2 electrical service units
1 cable clip

2 Tables
2 back panels
1 end panel
2 electrical service units
4 cable clips

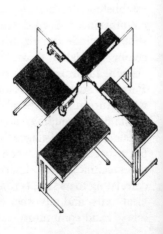

3 Tables
2 back panels
2 electrical service units
5 cable clips

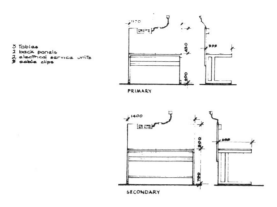

PRIMARY

SECONDARY

1 Tables
5 back panels
5 end panels
5 electrical service units
7 cable clips

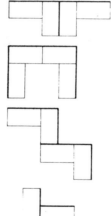

4 Tables
4 end panels
4 electrical service units
8 cable clips

OTHER TYPICAL ARRANGEMENTS

113

and help, while others may inspire new ideas. As school rolls continue to fall and as patterns of provision continue to change more consideration will have to be given to the use of existing spaces. Written information will also increase as these changes take place, and case studies can also provide ideas and help illustrate the potential and actual use of spaces.

The final stage is the consideration of detail, including clear, concise and consistent guiding of the library — using one house style, with a format which can be easily reorganised. This can then be linked to any other in-house productions, such as bibliographies and literature guides, helping to give the library an identity of its own. Colour is again important and should relate to furnishings. Visual displays including exhibitions should already have been considered, but pupils' and students' work should also be on display, and models, pictures and plants used to give warmth and colour so that the library has an intimate and welcoming atmosphere.

Having worked through all these stages, then a final and detailed report can be written. The extent of its detail will of course, depend on whether a new library is being built or whether existing space is being converted. It can then be discussed with the establishment and all those involved in the setting up and use of space, prior to action.

● Information — a selective list of relevant groups, institutes and associations

Colleges of Further & Higher
Education Group
Library Association
7 Ridgmount Street
London WC1E 7AE

Council for Educational Technology
3 Devonshire Street
London W1N 2BA

School Librarians Group
Library Association
7 Ridgmount Street
London WC1E 7AE

● Journals — a selective list

Building Bulletins
Department of Education and
Science
Elizabeth House
York Way
London SE1

Education
Longmans
Fourth Avenue
Harlow
Essex

Information Design Journal
Editor — Robert Waller
P.O. Box 185
Milton Keynes MK7 6BL

● References — a selective list of relevant books, reports and articles

Altherton, B. *Adapting spaces for resource-based learning.* London, CET, 1980.
American Association of School Librarians and Association for Educational Communications and Technology. *Media programs: district and school.* Chicago, American Library Association, 1975.
Carroll, F.L. and Beilke, P.F. *Guidelines for the planning and organisation of school library media centres.* Unesco, 1979.
Clare, R. J. I. 'The snowball effect: an account of a school library exhibition' in *School Librarian 27,* (3) September 1979, pp 224-8.
Council for Educational Technology. *Audio visual resources in secondary schools: their organisation and management.* London, CET, 1980.
Council for Educational Technology. *Learning resources in colleges: their organisation and management.* London, CET, 1981.
Davies, R.A. *The school library media program: instructional force for excellence.* 2nd ed. New York, Bowker, 1979.

Department of Education and Science. *Accommodation for the 16-19 age group: NAFE: designing for change.* London, DES, 1980. (Design Note 22).

Department of Education and Science. *Accommodation for the 16-19 age group: four colleges in 1980.* London, DES, 1980. (Design Note 23).

Ellsworth, R.E. and Wagner, H.D. *The school library: facilities for independent study in the secondary school.* New York, Educational Facilities Laboratory, 1963.

Focus on safety. London, CET, 1979.

Library Association, Colleges of Further and Higher Education Group. *College library standards: recommended standards for professional service and resource provision.* 3rd rev. ed. London, Library Association, 1980.

Library Association. *School library resource centres: recommended standards for policy and provision.* London, Library Association, 1970.

Library Association. *School library resource centres: recommended standards for policy and provision, a supplement on non-book materials.* London, Library Association, 1972.

Lickley, A. *Towards individualised learning for teacher education.* London, CET, 1977.

Pollet, D. and Haskell, P.C. *Sign systems for libraries: solving the wayfinding problem.* London, Bowker, 1979.

Reynolds, L. and Barrett, S. *Signs and guiding for libraries.* London, Bingley, 1981.

Smith, P. *Design of learning spaces.* London, CET, 1974.

Usherwood, B. *The visible library.* London, Library Association, 1981.

Planning pointers

●   Before making decisions   Visualise the space as part of the existing system or systems, or as a new area.

Decide on concept, e.g. year plan, closed access, or other combinations.

Ask planning questions. Produce an interim report. Include details of environment and users.

For a new space collect as much hard information as possible including costs.

●   Analyse and consult   Pupil and staff activities (singly and in groups).
a. Formal
b. Informal

●   Consider   Storage and display of materials including requirements.

Exhibitions and visual displays of materials.

Production of materials
a. Central
b. Local

Administrative and service areas.

User education needs, related to the curriculum.

Architectural and technical detail.

Visual support and design.

Then: Produce a final report.

●   Review   All plans and make modifications if necessary.

Storage of resources

The ways in which spaces are planned and utilised relate to access to materials, and the ways in which they are physically stored can facilitate this access. This access is part of the policy of the library resource centre, which has to stem from the parent community. The more complicated the access points and the greater the number of sequences, the greater will be the difficulties encountered by the user, and these will be compounded by the variety of locations in the catalogue. One of the first major decisions is that of whether to integrate such materials with others (books) on the open shelves, or to maintain separate sequences. These can be subdivided by format or interfiled as one non book sequence. It is possible to integrate and interfile some materials, but there are always exceptions (large kits, three dimensional objects) and so planning decisions are complex. It may be that some materials are archival in nature and fragile (such as rare maps or very fragile resource items) and so these will have to be treated separately from the points of view of both physical storage and access by the users. If access is to be relatively open, then the costs of constantly replacing materials, inevitable in any library, must also be considered. In any combination of arrangements, access, wear and tear, loss, misfiling and the need for clear guiding for the user must be considered. Space may dictate some storage methods, such as the transferring of large and unwielding posters into slides, so that they can be handled easily, and cause little damage to the originals. The catalogue must also supplement and extend information relating to materials, which may not be obvious from these external packaging. Browsing is difficult.

Storage of materials has to relate both to their physical nature, which could dictate the whys and wherefores of storage methods if they are subject to physical decay (such as microforms and film), if they need equipment to have a viable and immediate use as a resource (such as tapes), and if materials and equipment are both on open access. Damage to resources through constant handling is another factor, as is servicing of equipment which is in constant use. Other factors to be considered include the cost of custom made and specialised containers, the effectiveness of displaying the classification marks and location on the container, and if possible some indication of the contents if this is not clear. These points should be considered as part of the planned use of the resources, and the ease with which they can be loaned and shelved.

● Information — a selective list of relevant groups, institutes and associations

Aslib
3 Belgrave Square
London SW1X 8PL

Aslib
Audiovisual Group
Aslib
3 Belgrave Square
London SW1X 8PL

British Film Institute
127-133 Charing Cross Road
London WC2H 0EA

British Universities Film Council
81 Dean Street
London W1V 6AA

CLRS Reference Library and
Information Service
ILEA Centre for Learning Resources
275 Kennington Lane
London SE11 5QZ

Library Association Audiovisual
Group
7 Ridgmount Street
London WC1E 7AE

Microfilm Association of Great
Britain
Longman Group Ltd
6th Floor
Westgate House
The High
Harlow, Essex

UK Serials Group
Group Secretary
School of Librarianship
Technical College
Loughborough

● Journals — a selective list

Audiovisual Librarian
Audiovisual Groups of Aslib and the
Library Association
Library Association Publishing
7 Ridgmount Street
London WC1E 7AE

● References — a selective list of relevant books, reports and articles

Beswick, N.W. *Organising resources.* London, Heinemann Educational, 1975.
Boss, R.W. *Developing microform needing facilities.* Westport, Conn.,
    Microform Review, 1981.
Bourne, R. (ed.) *Serials librarianship.* London, Library Association, 1981.
    (Handbook on library practice).
Butchart, I. and Fothergill, R. *Non-book materials in libraries: a practical guide.*

London, Bingley, 1978.

Chibnall, B. *The organisation of media.* London, Bingley, 1978.

Currall, F.J. (ed.) *Gramophone record libraries: their organisation and practice.* 2nd ed. London, Crosby Lockwood, 1970.

Edridge, S. (ed.) *Non-book materials in libraries: guidelines for library practice.* Wellington, New Zealand Library Association, 1980.

Harrison, H. *Film library techniques.* London, Focal Press, 1973.

Harrison, H. (ed.) *Picture librarianship.* London, Library Association, 1981.

Hicks, W.B. and Tillin, A.M. *Managing multi media libraries.* New York, Bowker, 1977.

Malcolm, A.H. *The setting up of a resources centre: 1. basic ideas.* Glasgow, Scottish Educational Film Association, 1974.

Nichols, H. *Map librarianship.* 2nd ed. London, Bingley, 1982.

Saddington, G.H. and Cooper, E. *Audiocassettes as library materials: an introduction.* London, Audiovisual Librarian, 1977.

Teague, S.J. *Microform librarianship.* 2nd rev. ed. London, Butterworth, 1979.

Williams, B. and Fothergill, R. *Microforms in education.* London, Council for Educational Technology, 1977.

Planning pointers

- Establish a policy for non-book materials.

- Decide if materials can be organised physically as integrated resources, or organised separately.

- Establish criteria for packaging, place of use, equipment, and loans.

- Decide on physical arrangements:
  — separate sequences, e.g. print materials and non-print materials (both classified).
  — integrated sequences (as far as possible) of all print and non-print materials, regardless of format.
  — partial integration — placing non-book materials near print items whenever possible.
  —arrangement by format — subdividing all materials into physical format and then grouping them into classified order.

- Be consistent in storage methods. Make sure notes are available.

- Help and guide the user as much as possible. Make sure that the catalogue also helps and does not hinder.

- Be consistent and maintain a record of decisions made in the staff manual.

Production of resources

The production of resources for curriculum support is an area of concern, as so many inter-related elements are involved. In addition to the relatively simplistic element of physical production (the kind of equipment and its production capabilities), there are also those of curriculum design and planning, which determine the extent of teacher based resources and pupil based resources, the organisation and staffing hierarchy of production staff and their relationship to the library, the quality and presentation of materials in relation to learning needs, and the organisation and control of the materials once they are produced.

The historical aspects of the growth of the 'production industry' have their roots in the growth of the resource centre movement, helped to lead to the design of many an ill-starred classification or cataloguing scheme and now form part of a highly sophisticated aspect of school and college planning.

The design and planning of the curriculum depends on the school structure, and the ways in which this responsibility is perceived both by the Head or principal and by the local authority. This may be through a senior appointment, or through Heads of Departments, and the essential points concern the ways in which the librarian is involved in this planning structure, and the ways in which he or she is involved in communicating any decisions. In other words the librarian has to be involved, as a matter of policy, in the planning of the curriculum so that the resources provided reflect these needs (either commercially purchased or produced in-house) and the communication structure is important so that everyone is aware of what is being planned, plus what resources are available and where they are. This relates very clearly to the whole problem of determining the structure and hierarchy of the school in relation to its policies as discussed earlier. These will have an effect on the ways in which resources are used, the extent to which the production of materials is concerned with the management aspects of the college, and the extent to which production supports teaching and learning activities.

The staffing of any kind of production unit, and the servicing of equipment in relation to the planning and design of the resources are both important and difficult. Both have an effect on the cost of resource materials. The eventual responsibility for such staff may well rest with a senior member of the management team, but there have to be close links with the library so that resources are controlled and duplication and waste avoided. Inter departmental co-operation must form part of this communication structure, so that any central unit or planning takes into account departmental planning, and also any departmental production activities. The recent CET survey quoted in the bibliography was one attempt to rationalise the levels and responsibilities of those involved in the production of resources, as so many people are involved who professionally cannot be clearly slotted into existing teaching or librarianship career grades. It is important that librarians in the educational sphere have some understanding of the production methods available, so that they can contribute to planning decisions and assess quality, but even more important that they understand the educational reasons for the choice of production media. This of course should be determined by the effectiveness of a specific medium for the information which is to be conveyed and this in turn springs from the curriculum. Again the need for the inclusion of such training in the basic librarianship syllabus becomes apparent, but it is important also to build on this with other courses as and when the need arises. Many such courses come under the umbrella heading of 'educational technology', which is not concerned merely with hardware but with a more organised approach to teaching and learning, incorporating management, methods and media (including production), and is concerned with a deliberate systematisation of new courses, stemming from clearly defined objectives. The need for an understanding of learning processes, involving the interpretation of objectives into a design for learning and then into a formal syllabus with its resource implications, will make increasing demands upon the librarian. A familiarity with the work of Rowntree, Bloom and Gagne is an advantage, and an understanding of the competences which the learner (the pupils or student) needs to be able to use the resources available. The production of resources will supplement and complement both locally and nationally produced materials, and so the characteristics of the media used are important to understand in relation to the broad learning domains which have been defined. Local co-operative schemes may be involved both with curriculum design such as locally based vocational schemes, and also with the production of expensive resources, when equipment, raw materials and staffing expertise can also be shared.

The organisation and control of materials should be the responsibility of the librarian, and such organisation will of course vary in complexity of structure from school to school. As well as depending on and working within the overall management structure, the librarian will also have to consider the ways in which budgeting is carried out and the degree of autonomy in terms of finance enjoyed by departments. Decisions have to be made about centralised servicing and production agencies, or departmental services, and funding decisions will relate to these. The actual organisation of costing in relation to raw materials, purchased items, running costs and local authority support is not as crucial as the actual implementing of some organisation — everyone has to be aware of the system and should conform to it within the limits of reason, as otherwise there will be endless duplication and overlap. Hopefully master copies of materials will be held centrally and departmental holdings will also be listed centrally. Access to all resources to prevent a fragmentary approach to planning should be avoided. The design and degree of sophistication of the system used to control and organise materials, including location, access, booking systems and costing systems will of course depend on the size of the operation, the number and levels of staff available, the amount of central support, and the existence and support of local and authority networks.

● **Information — a selective list of relevant groups, institutes and associations**

Council for Educational Technology
3 Devonshire Street
London W1N 2BA

National Foundation for Visual Aids
National Audio Visual Aids Centre
Paxton Place Gipsy Road
London SE27 9SR

● **Journals - a selective list**

Audiovisual Librarian
Audiovisual Groups of Aslib and the
Library Association
Library Association Publishing
7 Ridgmount Street
London WC1E 7AE

British Journal of Educational Technology
Council for Educational Technology
3 Devonshire Street
London W1N 2BA

Coombe Lodge Reports
Further Education Staff College
Coombe Lodge
Blagdon
Bristol BS18 6RG

Reprographics Quarterly
National Reprographic Centre for Documentation
Hatfield Polytechnic
Bayfordbury
Lower Hatfield Road
Herts

● **References — a selective list of relevant books, reports and articles**

Beswick, N. *Resource-based learning.* London, Heinemann Educational, 1977.

Bloom, B. S. *Taxonomy of educational objectives. Handbook 1. Cognitive domain.* London, Longmans, 1956.

Bloom, B. S. *Taxonomy of educational objectives. Handbook 2. Affective domain.* London, Longmans, 1964.

Brown, J. W., Lewis, R. B. and Harcleroad, F. E. *AV instruction media and methods.* 3rd ed. Maidenhead, McGraw Hill, 1969.

Davies, I. K. *Management of learning.* Maidenhead, McGraw Hill, 1971.

Gagne, R. M. *Conditions of learning.* 2nd ed. London, Holt Rinehart and Winston, 1970.

Harris, N. D. C. *Preparing educational materials.* London, Croom Helm, 1979.

Mackenzie, N., Erant, M. and Jones, H. C. *Teaching and learning: an introduction to new methods and resources in higher education.* Paris, Unesco, 1970.

Rowntree, D. *Educational technology in curriculum development.* London, Harper and Row, 1974.

Thornbury, R., Gillespie, J. and Wilkinson, G. *Resource organisation in secondary schools: report of an investigation.* London, CET, 1979. (Working paper 16).

Willis, N. (ed.) *Teaching and learning support services. 1. Higher education.* London, CET, 1981.

Willis, N. (ed.) *Teaching and learning support services. 2. Further education.* London, CET, 1981.

Willis, N. (ed.) *Teaching and learning support services. 3. Secondary comprehensive, middle and primary schools.* London, CET, 1981.

Planning pointers

- Determine the management structure of the school in relation to curriculum planning and design.

- Make sure that the librarian is included in this hierarchy. Be involved in other and wider activities, such as resource committees and in-service training activities.

- Make sure that the management system which determines the production of resources includes the librarian.

- Co-operate in working out a system for the control and organisation of all in-house produced resources. Try and make this relate to any local schemes which exist. Make sure that the scheme is known and understood by all relevant people.

- Co-operate in rationalising the funding of departments within the school or college so that there is effective control over the production of resources.

- Use all training opportunities to understand further the relationship of physical resource materials to learning patterns and needs, and to teaching styles.

As with every other decision making processes, those that relate to classification and cataloguing follow a series of logical steps. The considerable literature on this area provides an enormous amount of advice and guidance on detail, which will not be reproduced here. Any service planned and managed within the library must relate to the user, and the bibliographical records must enable him or her to find information and resources (via author, title or subject), give a comprehensive listing of items, indicate their format (so that equipment can be located if necessary), and where they can be found. The user wants to know what resources are available, and where. The librarian also has to use the cataloguing and classification scheme to locate, check, evaluate and edit stock.

Planning can operate at the school, local and national level, and each has to be considered in turn. Before any planning decisions are made, certain facts have to be established, and the application of resulting criteria will help to ensure that the correct decisions are made. Firstly, at the local level, it is important to consider the immediate users as a total group (actual, and potential, if changes are planned), and to analyse what their real and perceived bibliographical needs are (e.g. planning citation services). This must firstly be carried out within the context of the school or college and then in the context of its wider relationships with other schools and colleges at a local and regional level. The size of the resource collection should be considered next, its physical and intellectual complexity, the number of sites where materials are located and the relationship of these to the central area. The number, complexity and use of any satellite resource collections should also be considered. The extent of any backlog, the need (or not) for a completely up to date set of records, and the need for bibliographies etc., are all important considerations. The range, need for local peculiarities and specialities, complexity of compilation and up-dating of any kind of subject index must be considered. The resultant mechanics and difficulties of maintaining an authority file follow logically from this set of decisions. The availability and professional levels of support staff, plus any access to additional staff within the school or college are criteria which affect decisions.

At the second and local level it is important to find out what authority services are available, what costs are involved, and what is the extent (in bibliographical terms) of such a service. Other facts relate to the variety of physical formats in which records can be produced, and if any other services (such as previewing and processing) are included. The format of any catalogue must take into consideration the necessary equipment to use it, and any costs involved in purchasing this, or problems of storage and availability.

Thirdly, at the national level (which may be applied regionally), it may be possible to use existing schemes, such as SWALCAP or BLCMP, tailored to the requirements of specific schools or colleges. At the national level the British Library offers its LOCAS services, which can also be tailored to specific needs. It is useful to determine if other services are included here, such as accessions lists, bibliographies, access to other bibliographical data bases (and the costs involved), access to documents and access to other subject data bases. Other criteria relate to the physical format of records (and their compatibility with existing records and equipment), their ease of use in conjunction with existing records, and delays, if any, in production. Because of the wide ability range of pupils in most schools, and the wide variety of approaches to the use of resources, it is also important to check if materials which particularly relate to a school collection, but which may be peripheral to or outside a bibliographical network, are included. These include computer software programmes, materials published by very small publishers or societies, some audio visual materials, and resources produced by ethnic and cultural groups.

From these considerations it should then be possible to decide if bibliographical records are to be generated within the school or college, if they are to be manually or computer generated, or if a regional or national service will be used. Once these major planning decisions have been made, it then becomes possible to determine the exact detail of the operation, both in terms of who on the staff will be responsible for the organisation and maintenance of the service, and the physical format, arrangement, and content of the records. All resources in the library act as information carriers, and the bibliographical treatment of these materials, and their classification, follow clearly established codes of practice. These relate to the intellectual and physical identification of the resource (including indicating if equipment is necessary to use the resource, the size/extent of the resource, and any other enriching element), its subject, and its location.

All the various cataloguing and classification schemes have been listed at the end of this section, and each has its own set of rules and examples. Again, it is crucial to maintain an authority file for any scheme that is used — other people may also have to maintain the service. If regional or national cataloguing services are used, and particular adaptations made, then these too should be noted (why and how) for future maintenance and planning. Decisions on the intellectual organisation of the catalogue as a tool for both staff and users (such as dictionary or classified catalogues and the treatment of materials in formats other than print) must also relate to earlier planning decisions.

Finally criteria and decisions can be applied to the staffing needs of the service, where it will be located, and what equipment is necessary. At a national level, a problem related to the bibliographical tracing of materials may present a problem as national control is still not complete. At present some non print materials are included in the national bibliographies and lists, and coverage is improving. The coverage still cannot compare to the bibliographical control for print materials (covered by copyright laws and legal deposit system), but sound recordings and films are relatively well documented. The existing bibliographies and bibliographical services and regional schemes have also been listed, but not the multiplicity of local and specialist guides which exist. They can be seen in local and regional libraries and bibliographical collections, or in neighbouring polytechnic and university libraries.

● Information — a selective list of relevant groups, institutes and associations

Arlis (Art Libraries Association)
Secretary — Graham Bullock
Hull College of Higher Education
Queens Gardens
Hull HU2 3DH

Aslib Computer Group
Aslib
3 Belgrave Square
London SW1X 8PL

Audiovisual Group
Aslib
3 Belgrave Square
London SW1X 8PL

Audiovisual Group
Library Association
7 Ridgmount Street
London WC1E 7AE

Bibliographic Information Systems
Officer
The Library Association
7 Ridgmount Street
London WC1E 7AE

Birmingham Libraries Co-operative
Marc Project (BLCMP)
Main Library
University of Birmingham
Birmingham B15 2TJ

Blaise Marketing
British Library
2 Sheraton Street
London W1V 4BH

British Film Institute
127-133 Charing Cross Road
London WC2H 0EA

British Institute of Recorded Sound
29 Exhibition Road
London SW7

British Library Bibliographic Services
Division
2 Sheraton Street
London W1V 4BH

British Records Association
Working Party on Audiovisual
Records
Public Record Office
Ruskin Avenue, Kew
Richmond TW9 4DU

British Telecom
Library Marketing Services, Prestel
Headquarters
Telephone House
Temple Avenue
London EC4Y 0HL

British Universities Film Council
81 Dean Street
London W1V 6AA

Cataloguing and Indexing Group
Library Association
7 Ridgmount Street
London WC1E 7AE

Educational Foundation for Visual
Aids
254 Belsize Road
London NW6 4BY

Educational Resources Information
Centre (ERIC)
National Institute of Education
1200 19th Street
Washington DC, 20208
USA

International Federation of Library Associations (IFLA)
Round Table on Audio Visual Media
C. Pinnion
Sheffield City Libraries
Sheffield S1 1XZ

National Sound Archive
29 Exhibition Road
London SW7

National Video Clearing House
32 Eveline Road
Mitcham
Surrey CR4 3LE

and

100 Layfayette Drive
Syosset
New York 11791
USA

Online Computer Library Centre (OCLC)
Lloyd's Bank Chambers
75 Edmund Street
Birmingham B3 3HA

Online Information Centre
3 Belgrave Square
London SW1X 8PL

Scottish Council for Educational Technology
Dowanhill
74 Victoria Crescent Road
Glasgow G12 9JN

Scottish Libraries Cooperative Automatic Project (SCOLCAP)
National Library of Scotland
George IV Bridge
Edinburgh EH1 1EW

South West Academic Libraries Cooperative Automatic Project (SWALCAP)
Wills Memorial Building
University of Bristol
Bristol BS8 1RJ

UK Serials Group
Group Secretary
School of Librarianship
Technical College
Loughborough

● **Journals — a selective list**

Audiovisual Librarian
Audiovisual Group of Aslib and the Library Association
Library Association Publishing
7 Ridgmount Street
London WC1E 7AE

British Universities Film Council Newsletter
British Universities Film Council
81 Dean Street
London W1V 6AA

Information Science Abstracts
Plenum Publications Corporate
233 Spring Street
New York
NY 10013
USA

Information Technology and Libraries
Library and Information Technology Association
American Library Association
50 East Huron Street
Chicago, Illinois 60611
USA

Online Review
Learned Information
Besselsleigh Road
Abingdon
Oxford OX13 6LG

Vine
Vine Office
Southampton University Library
Highfield
Southampton
Hants SO9 5NH

● Bibliographies — National

British Catalogue of Audiovisual
Materials. 1st experimental edition,
British. London, British Library,
Bibliographical Services Division,
1979.

British Catalogue of Audiovisual
Materials. Supplements. London,
British Library, Bibliographical
Services Division, 1980 and 1983.

● Bibliographies — Others

Audio Visual Materials for Higher
Education
British Universities Film Council
81 Dean Street
London W1V 6AA

British Catalogue of Music
London, British Library
Bibliographic Services Division
2 Sheraton Street
London W1V 4BH

British National Film Catalogue
British Film Institute
127-133 Charing Cross Road
London WC2H 0EA

British Universities Film Council
Higher Education Film and Video
Library
81 Dean Street
London W1V 6AA

British Universities Film Council
Higher Education Learning
Programmes Information Service
81 Dean Street
London W1V 6AA

Central Film Library
Chalfont Grove
Gerrards Cross
London SL9 8TN

Video Index
Link House
Croydon
Surrey

Video Source Book
Bookwise Video
Langham Trading Estate
Catteshall Lane
Godalming
Surrey GU7 1NG

● Bibliographies and other sources — listed elsewhere

Other sources of information, including lists of producers and publishers, are far too numerous to list here, but can be found in the standard bibliographies and Year Books listed in the text. Most large libraries also have collections of these bibliographies and lists of suppliers, and local lists of resource holdings will be happy to cooperate with smaller libraries over their use. Many local groups and centres also have lists of the holdings of local collections of materials, usually in a wide range of formats.

● References — a selective list of relevant books, reports and articles

Anglo American Cataloguing Rules. 2nd ed. London, Library Association, 1978.

Beswick, N. W. *Organising resources.* London, Heinemann Educational, 1975.

Butchart, I. and Fothergill, R. *Non-book materials in libraries: a practical guide.* London, Bingley, 1978.

Croghan, A. *A code of rules for, with an exposition of, integrated cataloguing of non-book media.* London, Coburgh, 1976.

Davinson, D. *Periodicals collection.* 2nd ed. London, Deutsch, 1978.

Dewey, M. *Abridged Dewey Decimal Classification and Relative Index.* 11th ed. New York, Forest Press, 1979.

Dewey, M. *Dewey Decimal Classification and Relative Index.* 19th ed. New York, Forest Press, 1979.

Dewey, M. *Introduction to the Dewey Decimal Classification for British Schools.* 3rd ed. (Revised and enlarged). B. A. J. Winslade. New York, Forest Press for the School Library Association, 1977.

Edridge, S. (ed.) *Non-book materials in libraries: guidelines for library practice.* Wellington, New Zealand Library Association, 1980.

Fairfax, O., Durham, J. and Wilson, W. *Audio visual materials: development of a national cataloguing and information service.* London, CET, 1976. (Working paper 12).

Ferris, D. *Learning Materials Recording Study.* London, CET. (Research and Development Dept. Report No. 5661).

Fleischer, E. and Goodman, H. *Cataloguing audiovisual materials: a manual based on the Anglo-American Cataloguing Rules II.* New York, Neal-Schuman Publishers Inc. London, Mansell Publishing, 1980.

Foskett, A. C. *Subject approach to information.* 4th ed. London, Bingley, Hamden, Conn., Linnet Books, 1982.

Furlong, N. and Platt, P. *Cataloguing rules for books and other media in primary and secondary schools.* Oxford, SLA 1976.

Gorman, M. *Concise Anglo American Cataloguing Rules.* 2nd rev. ed. London, Library Association, 1981.

Harrison, H. *Film library techniques.* London, Focal Press, 1981.

Harrison, H. (ed.) *Picture Librarianship.* London, Library Association, 1981.

Hunter, E. and Fox, N. *Examples illustrating AACR2.* London, Library Association, 1980.

International Federation of Library Associations and Working Group on the International Standard Bibliographic Description on Non-book Materials. London, IFLA, 1977.

International Video Yearbook. London, Blandford Press, 1981.

Library Association. Media Cataloguing Rules Committee. *Non-book materials cataloguing rules.* London, Library Association/National Council for Educational Technology 1973 (Working paper 11).

Non-book materials: the organisation of integrated collections. 2nd ed. Jean Weihs with Shirley Lewis and Janet McDonald, in consultation with the CLA/ALA/AECT/AMTEC Advisory Committee on the cataloguing of non-book materials. Ottawa, Canadian Library Association, 1979.

Olson, N. B. *Cataloguing of audiovisual materials manual based on AACR2.* Minnesota, Minnesota Scholarly Press, 1981.

School Library Association. *Cataloguing rules for books and other media in primary and secondary schools.* Oxford, School Library Association, 5th ed, 1976.

School Library Association. *Routines: managing a small school library.* Oxford, School Library Association, 1980.

Sears. *List of subject headings.* 12th ed. New York, H. W. Wilson Co, 1982.

Shifrin, M. *Information in the school library: an introduction to the organisation of non-book materials.* London, Bingley, 1973.

Swatridge, C. *A list of subject headings for school and other libraries.* Oxford, School Library Association, 1981.

Vickery, B. C. *Techniques of information retrieval.* London, Butterworths, 1970.

Weihs, J. *Non-book materials. The organisation of integrated collections.* Ottawa, Canadian Library Association, 1973.

Planning pointers

- Apply criteria in logical order working from the school or college outwards.

- Work in context, not in isolation.

- Establish the basic facts, including the bibliographical needs of the users, staff involved, costs, etc.

- Look at other local and national systems in operation, and draw ideas from examples of 'good practice'.

- Decide what scale of operation is necessary:

  Local — e.g., in-house and school or college based, using standard schemes of cataloguing and classification practice, and manually generating a catalogue.

  Local — e.g., in-house and school or college based, using standard schemes, but computer generated, if relevant equipment and expertise is available.

  Local — e.g., using regional (commercial) or authority schemes, and using school or college staff only to cope with 'extra' materials. Could be manually or computer generated, or a combination, depending on local conditions.

  National — e.g., utilising a national scheme and/or data base for local needs.

- Be familiar with technical developments and find out where to obtain advice.

- Be part of, or establish, a committee or working party to consider and support new developments in school.

- Decide on detail — physical format, arrangement, content of entries.

- Decide on staffing needs (present and future levels).

- Decide on working areas.

- Provide relevant equipment.

- Train the users in the use of the system, both library and teaching staff, as well as pupils and students. Integrate this system into curriculum planning whenever possible, and do not present it as an isolated skill.

Although computer software programmes are intrinsically yet another learning resource, they deserve some brief consideration as a discrete group of materials because they are currently at the developmental stage and are therefore associated with particular problems. (These are very similar to those that were associated with the developmental period of other materials in non print formats, such as video tapes.) Many of the 'teething troubles' evident in the early 1970s which related to such materials are beginning to be sorted out, and rather than embark on a complicated home-produced scheme it is preferable for school librarians eventually to adopt national practices (suitably edited as and where necessary). This will prevent a multiplicity of home-grown schemes (very confusing to the user) and also lay foundations for the users for access to other national bibliographical sources, whenever and wherever other information service points are used.

Present activities relating to computing software revolve around national plans as well as around local initiatives. At the national level, the British Library (via the British Catalogue of Audio Visual Materials) is trying to standardise and rationalise the bibliographical control of these materials, within the context of the chosen national system, e.g. the Dewey classification scheme and the use of the MARC tapes. The problems of indexing the materials (from the point of view of the needs of the user), and an indication of the level of programmes, are those that relate to all materials in bibliographies which are used in the educational context and which are produced to national standards. Links with the Microelectronic Education Programme should help in the process of the collection and standardisation of the listing of materials. These national initiatives are supplemented by national research projects, and particularly the CEDAR project (Computer in Education as a Resource) based at Imperial College, which has CET funding and which is acting as an 'interim' national information and dissemination agency. CEDAR is now involved in the SOCCS project (British Library and MEP funded) concerned with producing guidelines for the cataloguing of computer software, based primarily on AACR 2, hence its title, 'Study of cataloguing computer software'.

At another level there are many local initiatives, in some cases providing a similar service to the CEDAR project, but in a more informal manner, and at a very local level. Some are based in one school, college or polytechnic, while others are area based. Some of these local 'collectives' are concerned with the listing of local collections, satellite or departmental collections, specialist materials (e.g. teachers working with materials in a particular subject area), and the local dissemination of advice, information and exchange of experience. Access and the use of materials locally is also possible through the use of telesoftware equipment (e.g. the transmission of have access to programmes and data available in other parts of the country via Prestel also enhances this facility, and the first project will start at Hatfield Polytechnic next year.

The whole area also affects the use of materials in the curriculum, as local groups tend to produce local materials, but information on these materials is not disseminated at a national level, and so either they are not fully utilised, or they cannot be fully utilised as equipment is not compatible or available. However, materials which are, conversely, produced and then listed at a national level tend not to be as widely used as they should be, as they do not always relate closely to local needs and conditions. These problems affect the further production of programmes at all levels as local initiatives need support, and national initiatives also need to be seen as essential to curricular growth. The inter-linked problems of initial and in-service training are also vital elements as the design of software should stem from curricular design. The organisation of materials forms only one part of their use, once the principle of a standard bibliographic entry for all materials has been accepted. Thus organisation is a relatively minor part of the picture, as the extracting of the planned experience from the use of the programme is the vital element, as computer software programmes are utilised as just one more educational resource.

● Information — a selective list of relevant groups, institutes and associations.

Advisory Unit for Computer Based
Education (AUCBE)
Endymion Road
Hatfield
Herts.

Association of Computer Users in
Colleges of Further and Higher
Education
Computer Services Unit
North Staffordshire Polytechnic
Blackheath Lane
Stafford ST18 6AD

Bibliographic Information Systems
Officer
Library Association
7 Ridgmount Street
London WC1E 7AE

British Computer Society
13 Mansfield Street
London W1

British Library
P. Baxter, T. Cannon and P. Graddon
Research and Development
Department
Sheraton House
Great Chapel Street
London W1V 4BH

CEDAR Project (Computers in
Education as a Resource)
Information Officer
Imperial College Computer Centre
Exhibition Road
London SW7 2BX

CET Telesoftware Project
Burghleigh Teachers Centre
Wellfield Road
Hatfield
Herts

Central Programme Exchange
(Department of Computing and
Mathematical Sciences)
Wolverhampton Polytechnic
Wulfruna Street
Wolverhampton WV1 1LY

Computers in the Curriculum
Information Officer
Chelsea College Educational
Computing Section
522 Kings Road
London SW10 0VA

Council for Educational Technology
3 Devonshire Street
London W1N 2BA

County Links Access to Information
on Resources and Expertise
(CLAIRE)
W. J. K.Davies,
County Programmed Learning
Centre
c/o St Albans College
St. Albans
Herts.

Department of Industry
Ashdown House
123 Victoria Street
London SW1

Independent Schools
Microelectronics Centre
Charles Sweaten
Oundle School
Peterborough PE8 4EN

Institute of Information Scientists
Special Interest Group
CIBA-Geigy P and A Company
Industrial Chemicals Division
Tenax Road
Trafford Park
Manchester M17 1WT

Micro-Computers in Primary
Education
c/o Upwood School
Upwood
Huntingdon
Cambridgeshire PE17 1QA

Microcomputers in Secondary
Education (MUSE)
48 Chadcote Way
Catshill
Bromsgrove B61 0JJ

Microelectronics Education
Programme
Director — Richard Fothergill
Cheviot House
Coach Lane Campus
Newcastle NE7 7XA

National In-Service Training
Coordinator: Communications
Technology
Peter Wheeler (PETRAS)
Ellison Place
Newcastle Polytechnic
Newcastle Upon Tyne NE1 8ST

National In-Service Training
Coordinator: The Computer
Philip Russell
50 Tanygraig Road
Bynea
Llanelli
Dyfed SA14 9LH

National In-Service Training
Coordinator: Computer-Based
Learning
Mike Aston
8 Causeway Close
Potters Bar
Herts EN6 5HW

National In-Service Training
Coordinator: Electronics and Control
Technology
Graham Bevis
Ronsella
Lordswood
Highbridge
Eastleigh
Hants SO5 7HR

National In-Service Training
Coordinator: Information Retrieval
Ann Irving
Department of Library and
Information Studies
University of Technology
Loughborough LE11 3TU

National In-Service Training
Coordinator: Special Education
Mary Hope
Council for Educational Technology
3 Devonshire Street
London W1N 2BA

RML Users Group
(Research Machines Ltd)
c/o Peter Smith
Educational Computing Section
Chelsea College
552 Kings Road
London SW10

Schools Information Research
Project
Aslib
3 Belgrave Square
London SW1X 8PL

Study of Cataloguing Computing
Software
CEDAR
Imperial College Computer Centre
Mechanical Engineering Building
Exhibition Road
London SW7 2BX

Telesoftware and Education Project
M. St. J. Raggett
Faculty of Education Studies
Room A122
Brighton Polytechnic
Falmer
Brighton

University of London
Central Information Services
Senate House
Malet Street
London WC1E 7HU

● **Journals — a selective list**

CAL News
Council for Educational Technology
3 Devonshire Street
London W1N 2BA

CET News
Council for Educational Technology
3 Devonshire Street
London W1N 2BA

Computers in Schools
Hon. Secretary
Microcomputers in Secondary
Education (MUSE)
Bromsgrove B61 7BR

Educational Computing
Educational Computing Ltd
30-31 Islington Green
London N1 8BJ

ITMA Newsletter
ITMA Project Secretary
College of St. Mark and St. John
Derriford Road
Plymouth PL6 8BH

Online Magazine
Online Inc
11 Tannery Lane
Weston
Conn. 06883
USA

Online Review
Learned Information
Besselsleigh Road
Abingdon
Oxford OX13 6LG

Practical Computing
IPC
Oakfield House
Perrymount Road
Haywards Heath
Sussex RH16 3DH

Vine
Vine Office
Southampton University Library
Highfield
Southampton
Hants SO9 5NH

●   **References — a selective list of relevant books, reports and articles**

Alcock, M. 'The Learning Materials Recording Study: a joint British Library/Inner Education Authority research project' in *Audiovisual Librarian,* 5 (2), Spring 1979, pp. 59-64.

Burton, P. F. 'The microcomputer in the smaller library' in *Scottish Library Association News,* 16, 1980, pp. 175-8.

CEDAR. (Computers in education as a resource). *Evaluation of CBL: a bibliography.* London, CEDAR project, 1981.

Computer applications in libraries. Tape slide programme. London, British Council, 1980.

Department of Education and Science. *Micro-electronics programme — the strategy.* London, DES, 1981.

Directory of Training 1982. Enterprise House, Badgemore Park, Henley-on-Thames, Oxon RG9 4NR.

Gilchrist, A. *Minis, micros and terminals for libraries and information units.* London, Heyden, 1981.

Horsnell, V. 'Cataloguing computer software' in *Library Association Record, 84* (7/8) July/August 1982, p. 251.

Information Technology and Education. Milton Keynes, Open University, 1982.

Maddison, J. *National education and the microelectronics revolution.* Clevedon, Clevedon Printing Co. 1980.

Moore, N. (ed.) *On-line information in public libraries: a review of recent British research.* London, British Library, 1981. (Research and Development Report No. 5648).

Payne, A., Hutchings, B. and Ayre, B. *Computer software for schools.* London, Pitman, 1980.

Rushby, N. *An introduction to educational computing.* London, Croom Helm, 1979.

Planning pointers

● Be informed about national bibliographical developments.

● Be informed about national technological developments in relation to computers, as another educational resource.

● Co-operate with any local schemes which try to alleviate bibliographical and access problems.

● Also utilise such schemes to gain more personal expertise. Tap resources and ideas on classification schemes used for software in local institutions of higher education. Use any existing schemes (if applicable) until national coverage is complete.

● Add relevant programmes to the library stock, in consultation with teaching staff.

● Check that the equipment is available and compatible.

● Establish criteria for selection which relate to those used in the selection of printed and other materials.

planning the management and organisation of resources

	LEA structure and influence	Library services and support	Specific school or college structure	THE USERS
funding				
selection				
acquisition				
access, organisation of space and storage				
production				
bibliographic organisation and control				

7 Planning the staffing levels

The levels and number of staff are the final link in this particular planning chain. The information on the authority and its services (centralised support) will help determine the numbers of support staff at the clerical and technician level. There is obviously a need to maintain a service, but little point in providing staff to carry out routines which can be done elsewhere and at little or no cost. A reasonable standard of immediate maintenance (repairs, production etc.) is essential, but must relate to these centralised services. The individual library policy and services will determine staff requirements at the professional level.

There is an incredible amount of confusion and controversy over the staffing of library resource centres, but in this context only the staff under the direct control of the librarian are being considered. It is however important to relate to and consider what support staff the library has access to, either directly within the school or college or through the local authority, and which services such staff can provide. The maintenance and repair of equipment and the production of resources are areas where it is crucial to determine levels and extent of support. These also relate to the costing of services, as some will be 'hidden' within the authority structure, while others may have to be directly costed. The centralised production of resource and curriculum support materials is another factor to be considered in relation to staffing levels, together with the degree of autonomy within schools in the planning and production of resources.

If the librarian is involved in the recruitment of staff (as should be the case) then it is important to understand who is being recruited, what criteria are being used and what to look for. The same principles apply to all staff recruitment procedures, from ancillary or clerical help to experienced librarians. As with all similar procedures the first stage is the analysis of the facts which relate to a proposed or particular post, and the second an alteration in levels, hours, conditions etc., as a result of that analysis. The analysis includes looking at the level of any current or proposed post, asking if it needs to be maintained at this level, establishing the procedures for filling or altering the post, and finally considering the implications for the training and assessment of the person appointed.

The next stage consists of fleshing out the analysis — translating the vacancy into a job description from which a real person can be recruited. Such a description not only outlines the detail of the post, but places it in context so that any interested person is aware of the parameters. A job description will include general details of the post and the major duties involved, indicating the level (decided by the analysis), the title, qualifications required, and conditions of service and salary. From this description a detailed job specification can be made, showing whoever is recruiting what is required for the post in terms of education, qualifications, training, experience and an indication of motivation and personal qualities. This specification can also be used as a general check list when assessing the performance of staff at a later stage as it gives an indication of required standards. The final phase consists of the librarian (or whoever is responsible for recruiting) drawing up a set of criteria for the ideal person to fill such a post. These criteria are then used in selecting and rejecting for a short list, and selecting and rejecting at the interview stage. They relate to status, age, qualifications, training and experience, special skills or expertise which form part of the job, particular interest areas, and specific personal attributes.

If involved in the actual interview, then again the librarian should be aware of some of the basic points to follow. These include having clarified objectives, having all specific and general background information available, relating both to the post and to the authority, and a check list (mental or otherwise) of the main pointers in the job specification. The librarian should also be aware of the standard anti-discrimination laws. It is also important to remember to put the person being interviewed at ease, to plan the interview so that it is structured in a meaningful way, and to use a structured rating form. It is also important not to ask confused or double meaning questions, to be aware of one's own personality and of personal prejudices intruding or becoming apparent, to give the interviewee time to ask questions, and finally to make any relevant notes as soon as the interview is over and before any information is lost. The actual interview is a process of extracting information in this case from the interviewee, and using this information to make informed judgements (by the interviewer). This must be a fair and logical process so that all interviewees are given an equal chance to express their potential, which is another reason for the need to structure interviews carefully. Notes taken at interviews can also be used at a later date as part of job evaluation procedures. Job evaluation is a technique used by some authorities to determine the grading of posts and future upgradings. It is a procedure which can be 'analytical' or 'non-analytical' and each authority will have its own scheme, probably related to or part of a personnel department. Some authorities also operate appraisal schemes as part of an evaluative exercise for staff, and these can be linked to in-service training needs.

Once the staffing levels have been established, then they have to form part of a library structure, which in turn relates to the school or college management structure. When the structures are clear, then the ways in which decisions are made, through communication structures such as committees, become more effective. If such communication channels do not exist, then they can be logically constructed. Areas of responsibility within the library and the school relating to both teaching and support staff can be determined, and staffing support can be allocated. This will cover the purchase, design, production and use of materials in the context of the curriculum.

staffing decisions

```
┌──────────────────────────────────────────┐
│ Establish facts relating to existing and  │
│ planned provision of staff and resources  │
└──────────────────────────────────────────┘
                  ↓
┌──────────────────────────────────────────┐
│ Establish numbers of existing support     │
│ staff at direct or indirect levels        │
└──────────────────────────────────────────┘
                  ↓
┌──────────────────────────────────────────┐
│ Check extent of in-house production       │
└──────────────────────────────────────────┘
                  ↓
┌──────────────────────────────────────────┐
│ Analyse levels of specific posts          │
└──────────────────────────────────────────┘
                  ↓
┌──────────────────────────────────────────┐
│ Write job description                     │
└──────────────────────────────────────────┘
                  ↓
┌──────────────────────────────────────────┐
│ Draw up job specification                 │
└──────────────────────────────────────────┘
                  ↓
┌──────────────────────────────────────────┐
│ Establish criteria/person specification   │
└──────────────────────────────────────────┘
                  ↓
┌──────────────────────────────────────────┐
│ Appoint staff                             │
└──────────────────────────────────────────┘
                  ↓
┌──────────────────────────────────────────┐
│ Train staff                               │
└──────────────────────────────────────────┘
                  ↓
┌──────────────────────────────────────────┐
│ Replace when necessary                    │
│ Change posts/levels when necessary        │
└──────────────────────────────────────────┘
```

Association of County Councils
66a Eaton Square
London SW1

Association of Metropolitan
Authorities
36 Old Queen Street
London SW1

British Educational Administration
Society
Moray House College
Hollywood Road
Edinburgh EH18 8AQ

Centre for Library and Information
Management (CLAIM)
Department of Library and
Information Studies
University of Loughborough
Loughborough
Leics LE11 3TU

Centre for the Study of Management
Learning
School of Management and
Organisational Services
University of Lancaster
Lancaster LA1 4YX

Council for Educational Technology
3 Devonshire Street
London W1N 2BA

Educational Management
Information Exchange
National Foundation for Educational
Research
The Mere
Upton Park
Slough
Berks SL1 2DQ

Equal Opportunities Commission
Overseas House
Quay Street
Manchester

Industrial Society
Robert Hyde House
48 Bryanston Square
London W1H 1BQ

Institute of Personnel Management
IPM House
Camp Road
Wimbledon
London SW19 4UW

Institute of Training and
Development
5 Baring Road
Beaconsfield
Bucks HP9 2NX

Library Association
7 Ridgmount Street
London WC1E 7AE

Library Association
Colleges of Further and Higher
Education Group
7 Ridgmount Street
London WC1E 7AE

Library Association
School Libraries Group
7 Ridgmount Street
London WC1E 7AE

Local Authorities Management
Services and Computer Committees
3 Buckingham Gate
London SW1

● Journals — a selective list

Education
Longman
Fifth Avenue
Harlow, Essex

Educational Administration
Journal of the British Educational and
Administration Society
c/o Secretary
Head of Department of Educational
Management and Administration
Moray House College of Education
Edinburgh EH18 8AQ

LAMSAC News
Local Authorities Management
Services and Computer Committee
3 Buckingham Gate
London SW1E 6JH

Library Association Record (LAR)
Library Association
7 Ridgmount Street
London WC1E 1AE

Training Officer
Marylebone Press Limited
25 Cross Street
Manchester M2 1WL

● References — a selective list of relevant books, reports and articles

British Educational Equipment Association. *School books and equipment: a spending guide for local authorities, 1982-83* BEEA, 1982.

British Institute of Management. *Job evaluation: a practical guide for managers.* London, Management Publications, 1970.

Council for Educational Technology. *Learning resources in colleges: their organisation and management.* London, CET, 1981.

Council for Educational Technology. *Learning resources in secondary schools: their organisation and management.* London, CET, 1980.

Department of Education and Science. *The staffing of public libraries.* 3 vols. London, HMSO, 1976. (Library Information Series No. 7).

Education Year Book 1980. Councils and Education Press. London, Longmans, 1981.

Equal Opportunities Commission. *Job Evaluation schemes free of sex bias.* Manchester, EOC, 1981.

Filling a vacancy. Loughborough, CLAIM: 1981 (Management checklist 2).

Greenaway. *Making academic decisions in committees.* Bristol, Scedsip, nd.

Grummitt, J. *A guide to interviewing skills.* London, Industrial Society, 1980.

Induction. Loughborough, CLAIM, 1981 (Management checklist 4).

Industrial relations. Loughborough, CLAIM, 1981 (Management checklist 5).

Jones, N. and Jordan, P. *Staff management in library and information work.* Aldershot, Gower, 1982.

Library Association. *College libraries: recommended standards of library provision in colleges of technology and other establishments of further education.* 2nd rev. ed. London, Library Association, 1971.

Library Association. *Library resource provision in schools: guidelines and recommendations.* London, Library Association, 1977.

Library Association. *Recommended salary grades and conditions of service for school librarians.* London, Library Association, 1982.

Library Association. *School library resource centres: recommended standards for policy and provision, a supplement on non-book materials.* London, Library Association, 1972.

Library Association, Colleges of Further and Higher Education Group. *College library standards: recommended standards for professional service and resource provision.* 3rd rev. ed. London, Library Association, 1981.

London Computer Managers Year Book. London, LLGCM, 1982.

Mann, M. *Library manpower planning: a bibliographical review.* London, British Library, 1981. (British Library Research & Development Report No. 5614).

National Book Committee. *Public library spending in England and Wales.* London, National Book Committee, 1982.

Pearson, P. K. *Costs of education in the United Kingdom.* London, CET, 1977.

Plumbley, P. *Recruitment and selection.* London, Institute of Personnel Management, 1976.

Proctor, R. *Selection and recruitment of library staff.* Bradford, MCB Publications, 1982.

Recruitment interviewing. Loughborough, CLAIM, 1981. (Management checklist 3).

Savage, A. W. *Personnel management.* London, Library Association, 1977. (Library Association management pamphlet no. 1).

Tunley, M. *Library structures and staffing systems.* London, Library Association, 1979. (Library Association management pamphlet no. 2).

Vidal-Hall, J. *A guide to report writing.* London, Industrial Society, 1977.

Willis, N. (ed.) *Teaching and learning support services. 1. Higher Education.* London, CET, 1981.

Willis, N. (ed.) *Teaching and learning support services. 2. Further Education.* London, CET, 1981.

Willis, N. (ed.) *Teaching and learning support services. 3. Secondary, comprehensive middle and primary schools.* London, CET, 1981.

Planning pointers

- Establish the extent and levels of institutional and LEA support in technical, clerical and production areas.

- Plan staffing needs (library) in relation to the services planned or in operation.

- Check that proposed posts relate to the levels of professional work which is expected.

- Check that proposed posts are not duplicating services which could be provided centrally.

- Analyse proposed posts, provide job descriptions and job specifications.

- Determine criteria for selection.

- Check evaluation or assessment schemes available.

- Make sure that the resultant staffing structure fits into or correlates with the institution, the LEA and major developments (in terms of conditions of service and career prospects).

8 Personal strategies: some planning tactics

Having established the major framework for planning at an authority and school/college level, the next stage is to work out a planning strategy at a personal level. This is to make sure that there is no gulf between any development in the school or college and the library, so that the library is at all times fully integrated into the establishments. This is not achieved overnight and needs careful thought. There are three aspects to this area of strategic planning, each relating to the other:

(a) An involvement by the librarian in activities which help affect the establishment's policy, and which contribute to the use of resources within the context of this policy.

(b) Library resource centre planning — making sure that the library has a clear policy and a series of objectives which are made available to everyone, accepted by everyone and understood by everyone. This involves the production of clear and concise reports, which relate to policies and plans — what it is hoped to achieve, and annual reports — what has been achieved.

(c) Stemming from these objectives, a series of services and functions, again acceptable, available and understood by the school/college population.

It is possible to indicate some of the more detailed planning strategies under each of these broad headings, but all will vary enormously depending on local conditions.

At the first and 'integrated' level a librarian can be closely involved in the political and planning activities of the establishment by attending and, just as important, contributing to staff meetings, Heads of department meetings, subject/curriculum meetings and any other 'local' meetings. These can range from 'traditional' meetings to those organised by subject enthusiasts in minority areas, those building up new areas of the curriculum, resource committees, integrated studies committees, study skills committees, and others with differing titles, but all contributing to course provision. Librarians should also be involved in school focused in-service training activities for teachers. In some cases librarians will be asked to participate in team teaching activities or to contribute to classroom activities. All of these are two-way processes — they alert the librarian to curriculum development ideas, and feed back from the librarian information and ideas on resources, as an integral part of curricular activities. Stemming from this formal involvement can also be a considerable amount of informal involvement, such as joining in assemblies, house activities, bookshops, clubs, career talks and pastoral care activities.

The second and third aspects are concerned with the planning activities of the library resource centre, and careful planning and accurate communication are essential here, as spasmodic and erratic response to change does not inspire confidence, and the library must function on an equal footing with other departments. The policy of the library must be clearly stated, with its specific objectives, and the services and activities relating to these objectives. Make sure that these are not given entirely in librarianship jargon, or it will be difficult to get them accepted — state clearly and concisely what the library can do in terms of these services. For example, one objective will doubtless relate to 'providing a user education service'. In meaningful terms this means helping students to become independent users of information, through giving guidance on the layout of the library, the arrangement of material, use of reference books, finding material for projects and personal information, using information, assessing information and presenting it in a chosen final form.

In relation to these services, it is necessary to maintain a manual of decisions and procedures, so that this can be updated as procedures change, and also used as a planning framework for the next librarian in post, and as a training handbook for junior members of staff.

The librarian has to evolve some personal techniques and strategies to achieve all this, and again there will be local variations. But some general points apply to most situations. It is more effective to work with the committed and converted at first — they will influence others. Don't try and do too many things at once, but concentrate on the 'core' activities, usually committees or groups that are involved with finance or with a wide range of subjects and ages, such as study skills, integrated studies or heads of departments. Be aware of your position and role within a group, as observer, leader, participant or innovator, and plan your activities in relation to this perceived role. Also try and be aware of areas of change, which may be at the centre of opposing forces, but utilise these having once identified them. If you participate in committee meetings of whatever level, plan first why you need to be there, and what you will say. Prepare any information which has to be presented, and make sure that it is succinct and accurate. Make relevant notes if you are required to do so, and if asked to prepare any further information or carry out some research, make sure that this is done before the next meeting. The same basic principles apply to the writing and presentation of reports — be accurate, clear and logical. The structure and presentation of any reports by the librarian should of course relate to the intended audience.

154

Planning pointers

- Be involved in all relevant activities which relate to the activities of the school or college.

- Prepare policies and plans which clearly relate to specific services which the library can and will provide for the community it serves. These should include:
  long term policies and plans;
  short term policies and plans;
  detailed objectives and information on services — these should be as detailed as possible so that they can be discussed by everyone concerned, and be integrated into a 'whole school' policy;
  annual reports.

- Be familiar with the procedures (usually committees), within the school or college. Find out who is in the chair, secretary, etc, and how the system works.

- Obtain and read back copies of minutes and be familiar with previous decisions.

- If attending meetings be prepared. Make sure you have information relating to any relevant item on the agenda, and can speak to it (clearly and concisely!)

- If asked to present reports make sure that they are professional and accurate (plus short and concise).

- If necessary, lobby discretely before a meeting, and use the expertise and political knowledge of a senior member of staff to provide support.

- Be involved in other and 'wider' activities, such as resource committees and in-service training committees.

- Work with the mainstream, and not against it, at school and personal levels. Be aware of group relationships and areas of change and utilise these, as part of the library development, and as personal strategies.

Part 3
HOW TO USE RESOURCES

9   Resources for pleasure

Imaginative literature is integral to the planning, stocking and use of the library. The use of books and resources for purely personal pleasure permeates all levels of planning and use, and cannot be neatly pigeon-holed into one area of activity. This enrichment of the individual is at the heart of many other more formal activities. These develop in complexity as the pupil progresses through secondary and further education, but the firm base needs to be established, ideally in pre-school days. The use of books and resources at this personal level has implications across the curriculum, as so many other related activities stem from it. Once established, the habit of reading for personal pleasure is hard to lose, supported not only through the library and teaching staff, but also through the organisation of book clubs and bookshops. School support can compensate to some extent for any social deprivation and lack of home support.

The whole broad concept of 'learning to learn' is a process of discovery, including the crucial discovery of language skills. The core 'communication' skills, listening, speaking (talking), reading and writing, are acquired either through formal methods or through a variety of informal experiences. Amongst these skills, the ability to read is the key to many crucial activities, as it is related to self, and thence to the 'life and social skills arena'. Reading in itself is a collection of 'sub-skills' ranging from primary skills, to those of comprehension, evaluation and appreciation, which in turn are part of a myriad of other activities in life. Hence the vital importance of reading.

Children need to be able to read to develop their imaginative senses, important to the decisions they will make later, to be able to exploit materials available, to participate in imaginative experiences, and to formulate ideas. The ability to identify and locate information as part of their individual intellectual growth is also important, as the process of refining and building on previous understanding takes place. Imaginative literature provides a structure for development, as within the context of plot, pattern and rhythm the child can pursue his or her own dreams and a sense of critical awareness. This can be important in later years, particularly so for pupils who choose to 'opt out' of the formal aspects of the educational process. While this personal exploration and development is taking place through reading and the use of books, a sense of organisation (pagination, index, chapter structures and consistent headings) is also being fostered, which can lead on to a direct search for information. This can help encourage critical awareness. In turn this leads on to the ability to cope with problem solving exercises and the ability to plan, and again relates directly to the so-called life and social skills. Spelling techniques can be acquired, as can an awareness of poetic patterns leading to an expansion of individual writing styles, later enabling a child to write personal poems or stories, expressing very intense and private feelings, or to write about particular interests. All these help to develop the child's linguistic skills. For those from minority cultures this addition to some oral cultures may be especially important. Personal perceptions may also be fostered — a child can help select books for the library, or criticise those in stock, thus adding to his own sense of achievement and of making a contribution to the school. Those of differing abilities can work together or read together in a library with a unified sense of purpose, which can also help to foster a sense of planning and the concepts of order and structure.

The outcomes of reading are many and varied, changing from session to session, child to child, and environment to environment, and they can be said to form a 'hierarchy of exploitation'. This is a long term evolutionary process, growing from the basic skills to an aesthetic appreciation of language. Reading for pleasure, as one part of this, should not and cannot realistically be seen in isolation, but as part of the school language policy, involving the school librarian, as a crucial member of this policy making team. Policies affect the ways in which committees and departments function, and also affect the management of resources. These in turn affect the stocking of the library, including the level of materials, the relationships with departments (and departmental literature collections and reading schemes), the use of such collections in relation to centrally held stock, and department and central policies for the purchase of materials. There are also implications for the production of book lists and support materials — a variety of lists can be produced, including schematic or thematic approaches. These lists can cover current topics of concern, subjects of special interest, or particular developmental skill areas. It is crucial that the planning and co-operation involved in these activities operates across the curriculum, and that the librarian is central to them. It is important to liaise inside the school or college with those who have pedagogic skills, and with members of the staff with relevant subject expertise. Pupils can also contribute to these activities, and many have considerable subject knowledge of topics near and dear to their hearts.

If an effective school policy is formulated, then the library and the librarian form an integral part of this. Every school, hopefully, should at some point devise a systematic policy for the development of 'reading competence in pupils of all age and ability levels' (*A Language for Life*, HMSO, 1975, Chairman, Sir A. Bullock.). The report stressed the need for a language policy to be developed across the curriculum and integrated into all subject areas. The importance and central role of the library has been supported at a national level, as has the importance of the librarian not only by Bullock but by earlier reports also, including the Board of Education Reports of 1921 and 1941. However despite the 'official' support of such reports and considerable research, it is clear from the recent work of Lunzer and Gardner, and others, that reading is not occupying the central role in pupils' personal lives and in the curriculum that it should, and that far more work needs to be done in this whole area, again calling for closer co-operation between all those involved — teachers, librarians, the media, administrators and publishers, among others. Use of books can form the basis for so many other essential activities, including self development, language skills, evaluation skills and self sufficiency, and should be integral to the life of each child.

Policies cannot just be written down and left to stagnate, but in any educational establishment need to be reviewed, revised, adjusted and changed, as planning strategies and processes (content and method) evolve. Such a principle also applies to a whole school policy concerned with reading. All those in school must be aware of existing practice and informed of subsequent changes, so that individual and departmental planning is part of an informed and coherent whole. Teachers need to be informed of new developments and new materials so that they can make effective choices and decisions, even more important as resources decline. Librarians have a vital role here. Both teachers and librarians need to be involved in exploiting literary and information sources to the pupils, from the basic use of reference materials to the use of abstracts and on-line data bases. As methods, materials and ideas in this vast area are constantly changing, schools and colleges need to be informed of these changes, and will themselves then change. The librarian, as an integral part of the system, has to act as an agent for change and as an information source, and to provide and work with in-service training activities. The library is thus one part of the whole system (the school) in the classical sense, in that it functions on its own, but is also related to other parts of the school, which in turn relates to the local area and the national changes.

As library skills and reading permeate so many areas of a child's personal and school life, the librarian also has to carry his or her planning and liaising activities to other areas and agencies outside the school. These extend to local public libraries, community groups, political groups, and those involved in various social activities. The extension of reading schemes and other holiday activities all hinge around fully utilising the resources available. Local expertise both in and out of school can be utilised in the translation into and from mother tongues, the writing down of traditional stories from other cultures, story telling, and in the publication of reviews of materials in other languages. Links with both the local and national media

161

and co-operation with them are important. The role of the library through co-operation with radio and television can be extended through the provision of mother-tongue language materials, literacy materials, study skills materials, basic information on civil rights, and information to support programmes on personal and educational counselling. Links with the media are also important both for stimulation and personal enrichment, arousing personal interest as a result of serialisation of books. Library support and organisation of materials as an extension of off-air historical or scientific programmes can extend beyond the provision of basic texts or reference books, and can be used to encourage the reading of books supporting a theme, or can guide pupils and teachers to other resources. Links with the producers of programmes need to be taken further, and there is enormous potential for librarians to initiate new programme ideas, support ideas with practical advice, and develop local initiatives on a co-operative but equal basis. Each profession has much to give and learn from the other, and both need an awareness and understanding of both the potential and the actuality of each of these services. Volunteer reading schemes (as initiated through Capital Radio) also help to encourage reading for pleasure. This enriching process, through illustrating the place of literature and personal reading within a subject area, can be of great value to pupils who may have previously rejected any opportunity to read for personal pleasure, and can also be used to support all areas of the curriculum.

Further knowledge relating to the individuals' use of books and information sources is needed although there are many developments in this area, with a considerable amount of research taking place. On the other hand a great deal still remains to be investigated. Much more needs to be known, for example, about the personal inter-action between the individual child and the written text, how information is obtained and then represented, how it is selected, its relationship to other known units of information, and the relationship of the book to the child's own experiences, or lack of them. The importance of and effects of visual literacy, environmental influences, the 'systematic' approach to reading, the ways in which problem solving patterns are built up, and the ability to follow instructions (life skills) all need to be considered. The interpretation of poetry, and how language ability can be effectively assessed, also need further research. The needs of teachers in training, and their understanding of the role of literature with its associated problems, areas of expertise, and research should also be considered. The whole area of the new technology and the transmission of information, in conjunction with a very personalised activity such as reading, has also yet to be considered in any depth. The Assessment of Performance Unit at the DES has begun to look at the area of linguistic abilities partly as a response to the need for evolving a method of assessment, within the current context of 'accountability' in local government. This is however only one initiative, and there are many other areas yet to be explored within the context of rapid social and technological change.

Book Marketing Council
Publishers Association
19 Bedford Square
London WC1B 3JE

Books for Students
Junior Bookshop Department
Cattershall Lane
Godalming
Surrey

Booksellers Association
154 Buckingham Palace Road
London SW1

Bookworm Club
Freepost
Cumbernauld
Glasgow G68 0BR

Centre for Language in Primary
Education (ILEA)
Sutherland Street
London SW1V 4LH

Centre for the Teaching of Reading
School of Education
University of Reading
Reading

Federation of Children's Book
Groups
6 Cavendish Court
Park Road
Eccleshill
Bradford

International Board on Books for
Young People (IBBY)
British Section
National Book League
Book House
45 East Hill
Wandsworth
London SW18 2QZ

National Association for Multiracial
Education
48 Lewisham High Street
London SE13

National Association for Remedial
Education
Central Office
2 Lichfield Road
Stafford ST17 4JX

National Association for Teaching
English
108 Thornhill Road
Edgerton
Huddersfield
Yorks HD3 3 AU

National Book League
Book House
45 East Hill
Wandsworth
London SW18 2QZ

Publishers Association
19 Bedford Square
London WC1B 3JE

Puffin Club
Penguin Books Ltd
Harmondsworth
Middx.

Red House Children's Book Club
Industrial Estate
Station Lane
Witney
Oxfordshire OX8 6XQ

Scholastic Book Clubs
161 Fulham Road
London SW3 6SW

School Bookshop Association
1 Effingham Road
London SE12 8NZ

School Bookshop Scheme
W.H. Smith & Son
c/o Mr. J.A. Cettemull
10 New Fetter Lane
London EC4A 1AD

United Kingdom Reading Association
c/o Edge Hill College of Higher
Education
St. Helen's Road
Ormskirk
Lancs

Volunteer Reading Help (Capital
Radio)
c/o ILEA Centre for Language in
Primary Education
Sutherland Street
London SW1V 4LH

● Journals — a selective list

About Books for Children
Federation of Children's Book
Groups
A. Wheaton & Co. Ltd
Exeter

Children's Literature Abstracts
Children's Libraries Section of IFLA
Tan-y-Capel
Llanbrynmair
Powys SY19 7BB

Children's Literature in Education
Agathon Press Inc
49 Sheridan Avenue
Albany
New York 12210
USA

Dragons Teeth
National Committee on Racism in
Children's Books
240 Lancaster Road
London W11

English Magazine
ILEA English Centre
Sutherland Street
London SW1

Growing Point
Margery Fisher
Ashton Manor
Northampton NN7 2JL

Material Matters
Hertfordshire County Library
Services
County Hall
Hertford SG13 8EJ

Multiracial Education
National Association for Multiracial
Education
48 Lewisham High Street
London SE13

Reading Today International
International Reading Association
800 Barksdale Road
P.O. Box 8139
Newark
Delaware 19711
USA

School Bookshop News
School Bookshop Association
1 Effingham Road
Lee London SE12 8NZ

School Librarian
School Library Association
29/31 George Street
Oxford

Writers' and Readers' Publishing Co-operative
144 Camden High Street
London NW1 0NE

Signal
The Thimble Press
Lockwood
Station Road
South Woodchester
Stroud
Gloucestershire

● **References — a selective list of relevant books, reports and articles**

Anware, M. *Who tunes in to what? A report on ethnic minority Broadcasting.* London, Commission for Racial Equality, 1974.
Barnes, D. *From Communication to curriculum.* Harmondsworth, Penguin, 1976.
Britton, J. *Language and learning.* Harmondsworth, Penguin, 1970.
Butler, D. *Babies need books.* London, Bodley Head, 1980.
Chambers, A. *Introducing books to children.* London, Heinemann, 1973.
Chambers, N. (ed.) *The signal approach to children's books.* London, Kestrel, 1980.
Children's Books of the Year: 1980. Selected and annotated by Barbra Sherrard-Smith. London, National Book League, 1981.
Clark, M. M. *Young fluent readers.* London, Heinemann Educational Books, 1976.
Curriculum and examinations in secondary schools. Report of the committee of the secondary school examination council appointed by the President of the Board of Education. London, HMSO, 1941. (Chairman Sir Cyril Norwood).
Department of Education and Science. *A language for life.* HMSO, 1975. (The Bullock Report).
Healy, M. and Marland, M. *Language across the curriculum: a selection of books for secondary school teachers.* London, National Book League, 1979.
Heather, P. *Young people's reading: a study of the leisure reading habits of 13-15 year olds.* Sheffield, CRUS, University of Sheffield, 1981. (CRUS occasional paper 6).

Heeks, P. *Choosing and using books in the first school.* London, Macmillan Education, 1981.

Huck, C. S. *Children's literature in the elementary school.* London, Holt, Rinehart and Winston, 3rd revised, 1979.

Hunter-Grundin, E. and Grundin, H. U. *Reading: Implementing the Bullock Report.* Ward Lock Educational, 1978.

Ingham, J. *Books and reading development: the Bradford Book Flood Experiment.* London, Heinemann Educational, 1981.

Inglis, F. *The promise of happiness: value and meaning in children's fiction.* Cambridge, Cambridge University Press, 1981.

Lake, S. *Television's impact on children and adolescents.* Phoenix, Oryx Press, 1981.

Language performance in schools: primary survey report no. 1. London, HMSO 1981.

Lunzer, E. A. and Gardner, K. (eds) *The effective use of reading.* London, Heinemann, 1979.

Marshall, M. R. *An introduction to the world of children's books.* Aldershot, Gower, 1982.

Marshall, M. R. *Libraries and the handicapped child.* London, Deutsch, 1981.

Meek, M., Warlow, A. and Barton, G. *The cool web.* London, Bodley Head, 1977.

Merritt, J. *Developing independence in reading.* Milton Keynes, Open University, 1977.

Moon, C. and Raban, B. *A question of reading.* London, Ward Lock, 1975.

Obrist, C. *How to run family reading groups.* Ormskirk, United Kingdom Reading Association, 1981.

Open University. *Language in education: a source book.* London, Routledge and Kegan Paul, in association with Open University Press, 1972.

Smith, F. *Reading.* Cambridge, Cambridge University Press, 1978.

Southgate, V., Arnold, H. and Johnson, S. *Extending beginning reading.* London, Heinemann Educational for Schools Council, 1981.

Teaching of English in England, being the report of the Departmental Committee appointed by the President of the Board of Education to enquire into the position of English in the educational system of England. London, HMSO, 1921.

Vincent, K. *A survey of the methods by which teachers select books.* Sheffield, CRUS, University of Sheffield, 1980. (CRUS occasional paper 3).

Whitehead, F. et al. *Children and their books.* Schools Council Research Studies. London, Macmillan Education, 1977.

Whitehead, F. et al. *Children's reading interests.* London, Evans Methuen, 1975.

Planning pointers

- Establish if there is a school reading policy. Is it formally written down? Contribute to any policy as and when amendments and alterations are made.

- Be involved in all activities that are concerned with reading developments, both at formal and informal levels.

- Co-operate with your local public library and its activities.

- Co-operate with all other local agencies involved in encouraging reading, both in the school situation and other voluntary activities.

- Be informed about national developments and reports. Contribute to any committee within school or college which may be formed as a result of these.

- Be informed about the whole spectrum of skills and ideas that are connected with reading in the widest sense (i.e. from primary school reading to literary appreciation).

- Make sure that the library responds to new initiatives at a policy level, and also responds to new ideas presented by pupils or teachers.

- Maintain a stock which reflects new ideas and thoughts, and support teachers with information on changes and practice.

10   Resources for learning

The exploitation and effective use of library resources can be seen to operate on a number of levels, to some extent hierarchical, but at the same time inter-dependent, and each requiring clear planning. All must stem from the curriculum, and not from physical resources as isolated elements, and this concept is fundamental to all planning and strategies. All planning must link with and relate to reading policies and learning to learn policies.

This series of levels can be said to form such a hierarchy, beginning with an introduction to the basic physical layout of the library, and the guiding and arrangement of resources within this space. Stemming from this should be an introduction to the use of basic resource materials, including encyclopaedias and dictionaries, an introduction to the concepts of classification, and an understanding of the idea of the library as a resource within the establishment. The integration of information skills into all school and library planning, as part of a total 'learning to learn' policy within the whole school, forms the next difficult stage. This in turn forms the foundation for the individual pupil to become an independent learner. Extra-curricular activities form the fourth level, including the provision of book shops and book clubs, and the fifth level should be concerned with the widening of library activities into the local community and into national developments. The carrying out of the first three levels must be seen as crucial activities, leading into the fourth and fifth levels, which should be affected as and when possible.

Level 1 Orientation exercises

The exploitation of the physical area of the library (in addition to its resources) logically forms the first stage of student guidance. The planning of space has already been considered, but the grouping and design of furniture, use of posters, plants, and ease and pattern of movement are also important. The use of signs and guiding is also very important, as part of the evolution of a 'house style', contributing to a logical approach towards using services within a school (which may need advertising), and the finding of information by both staff and students. Good results can be achieved through careful and integrated planning, and do not require either expensive materials or large numbers of staff. Exhibitions and display areas play their part in exploiting resources, and can be thematic, of local interest

resources for learning: priority levels

must

All students MUST be competent in basic

Listening
Speaking
Reading
Writing
Numeracy
Visual proficiency

and MUST be able to cope with planning,
particularly the identification of a problem
(possibly with help)

should

Advantageous to be able to cope with:

ORGANISATION of resources—
how information is arranged

MANAGEMENT of resources—
how to use information
e.g. extract it for personal use and move towards
autonomy — presentation

could

Be able to utilise networks of resources and
information beyond school and college boundaries
Life skills
leads to AUTONOMY

and importance, or linked to community and cultural activities. Pupils can also participate in these activities and many bring their own work or treasures to help excite interest. Book clubs and book festivals are also similar activities. Story telling, visiting authors, and similar activities all help to exploit the materials in the library and can help make it a pleasant physical setting for pupil and student activities, at a very personal level.

It may be helpful if some materials, such as reference books or overnight loans, are colour coded, to indicate their use as a specific resource. Such colour coding can be carried through to all library publicity, so that the 'house' style does emerge in a variety of ways. This introduction to the physical space which comprises the library, and the people within it, is the first stage in the potential full use of its resources. Part of this public relations exercise should also include an introduction to the services provided. This introductory exercise should also be used to stress the importance of the library and its staff as a central resource, and should be carried out at appropriate times, such as at the beginning of each session, to new groups of students, and to visiting staff. All publicity materials should include details of locations, hours, staff names, and any special collections or services which are provided. Many are under-used merely because no-one knows they exist. Services have to be promoted so that they can be evaluated, and changed in response to need and use. Again the way in which such information is presented is crucial — the librarian has to determine and plan for the information needs of a specific group of users.

This orientation process can be used to demonstrate the variety of ways in which the library can support staff and students, and some indication of the extent of the resources available should be given, related to the fact that such resources are produced or selected and organised within a system, and the system is designed to help the user. Brief details of any classification scheme used could be given at this stage, backed up by simple handouts, and supported of course by good planning, layout and guiding. Also very brief guides could be made available indicating the skills which will be involved in using resources within levels two and three, including the use of systems, including alphabetical/numerical order and the finding and presenting of information. It is helpful to reinforce these concepts at opportune times, such as at the beginning of new courses, or new terms, so that the concept of an organised physical area, providing a supportive system of resource provision, guidance and use is maintained.

Level 2 Planning the integration of resources: policies and strategies

The second level involves integrating the use of resources within the library services at policy making levels and so should eventually enable students to relate to and exploit resources for their individual needs. The basic and essential ability to extract information and use materials for a variety of purposes forms one strand in the encouragement of pupils and students to become autonomous learners. It enables them to adapt to change within a variety of individual situations, and to be able to cope with the demands of these situations. Such a state of independence is of equal value to the primary school child or the Ph.D. student. Policies and management structures affecting resources can be made or changed, but the central concept of student autonomy remains constant. Curricular decisions are arrived at as a result of planning around the ways in which children learn. Curricular content and methodology determine acquired skills, and these skills provide and support the ability to learn how to learn, and so to become an independent learner. If a school has decided to support this philosophy then policies and planning must support it throughout the school structure.

The resultant way in which the curriculum is organised reflects differing patterns of both learning and teaching and so of resource use. Resource based teaching (the most common), resource based learning (talked about frequently but difficult to achieve), computer assisted learning and computer assisted instruction, require print based activities, non print based activities, multi-resource based activities, and other combinations. These differing patterns can be extended and used outside formal institutional activities, and become part of community education, open learning and distance learning activities, all of which support the individual learner. All depend on resources, and so on the library to organise and exploit these, once their use has been planned as part of an integrated school or college exercise. Differing resource patterns of use are also formed as a result of differing attendance patterns, for example, small remedial groups, school and college links, and the larger classes found in some subject areas. These patterns affect in turn the resource needs of the teaching staff, who need materials for resource based teaching, for resource based learning and for adding to their subject and professional knowledge.

The advantage of individualised instruction is that the student becomes the focus of the exercise, the teacher is free to become the manager of the learning situation, and resources and planning support individual pupils. Students can proceed at their own pace and at their own level, and so have a greater degree of autonomy. The emphasis currently being placed on the individual is also reflected in the growth of open learning systems (at college, local and national levels), in which the ability of students to use resources at these second and third levels is crucial, if they are to be able to manage such situations. If curricular objectives within a school are matched to the objectives of the learning materials (either commercial or locally produced) then the librarian must be involved in the preliminary planning stages, so that no conflicting advice or methods are used.

In turn these activities all have training and production implications. Teaching staff need to be trained in the design and production of curricular support materials and their use. It is difficult to use efficiently a poorly designed and executed worksheet or project pack, in just the same way that it is difficult to use a poorly designed and presented book. The materials themselves have to be placed in the context of the curriculum so that materials for project work are not just personal expressions of interest by the teacher or librarian. Support in the training area can come from the library and from local support (teachers' centres etc.) and national agencies, all basically concerned to exploit and use resources to meet pupil and student needs. Once individual teachers are familiar with philosophies and strategies, then they can share their expertise within the school and so help to form a corporate policy, which supports individual pupils through good strategies.

The library and librarian will be at the centre of most of these activities, both in selecting, acquiring, organising and evaluating resources, and in providing a dissemination service tailored to institutional and individual activities. The services resulting from these needs and activities will also support individuals, ranging from the provision of materials to opening hours, and from formal orientation and induction activities to individual tuition. All however can be broadly grouped under the wide concept of organising resources as part of the learning to learn process.

Services must form part of a system which provides this individual support, and which is flexible. As the curriculum changes, so these services too must change, even in such basic areas as the provision of an overnight loan system, project loans, quick reference materials, changing satellite collections, class loans, tutorial group loans and field trip loans. If these services are to support the curriculum at institutional and individual levels, the importance of determining policies and structures at the initial planning stage again becomes apparent.

The design of information also has to be considered. This concept follows logically from the need to provide good basic physical guiding of the library, and an advertisement of its services, so helping students to identify with the library as the initial stage of a planned process. The design of the information within the library, and the relationships between the librarian and the materials follow logically. This relationship is concerned with materials that are designed as an integral part of exploiting resources, or of producing materials for a particular need. It does not include materials whose design has been determined by a commercial publisher, as many constraints and ideas are then involved.

The way in which information is presented has a crucial impact on its use, and the librarian has a considerable responsibility here. Many librarians already produce materials, such as book lists, catalogues etc., and so are familiar with some of the problems involved. It is important to be familiar with some of the processes, so that information and its presentation can also be a form of support for the individual pupil or student.

The initial planning decision involves the identification of need, so that the librarian establishes why information has to be made available, what information, for whom and at what levels. All these factors can be grouped together under one heading as 'the problem'. The constraints imposed by money, availability of reprographic equipment, staff, expertise, range of production services and range of other design expertise available must also be considered. Text needs to be structured and displayed effectively to have real validity as part of the design of information. The constraints imposed by the chosen 'house-style', both in the library and in other areas of the school or college are also important, so that a consistent approach is maintained.

The librarian then has to analyse the information which is required, and interpret this for the number of staff who will carry out the work. If there are staffing problems then the librarian may have to do the work alone, but the analysis, consideration of constraints, and interpretation of the material are still essential. Format, colour and other physical aspects will follow from the information itself. Only too often detail is decided before any other points have been considered, so that the planning process is reversed. This accounts for some of the inexplicable bibliographies, jargon ridden worksheets on how to use a catalogue, and complex flow charts (among others!).

The publication of book lists is one activity in which librarians are frequently involved, and these would in many cases be more effective if the information or books to be listed were first isolated, then the target audience determined and the level of user, then the curricular links to be emphasised, and finally the interpretation and consideration of the production aspects. Such lists can be in chronological order, alphabetical order, annotated or in any other form, comprehensive or selective, but these decisions relate to the initial planning stages, and should not be imposed at the end of the process as a result of decisions imposed by physical constraints.

Level 3 Learning to learn: policies and strategies

The effective use of library and other resources and the acquiring of information skills can now be seen to be a major part of the learning to learn process, and one which tries to guide the pupil or student towards a certain state of independence. Other aspects of this process include self organisation, listening skills, reading strategies and question formulating, so that pupils can increasingly manage their individual learning situations, as they become increasingly aware of and informed about the learning process. Teachers and librarians have to focus more and more on the process of learning, so that planned strategies complement, and do not conflict with these processes. It forms part of the whole process of curriculum innovation, and so involves the whole school in the formulation of policies and strategies to support such innovation. Once these policies have been determined, then the support strategies can be worked out. The library and the librarian have a major role to play at this level in the provision of information skills expertise, as part of the whole school policy. The librarian also has to have a clear perception of his or her role to do this effectively, and the school too has to understand this role. Again there are implications both for initial and in-serivce training, so that librarians working in the education sector have an adequate background and can respond to the changing institutional needs. The pupil or student must be able to perceive the need for this school support, and to relate the expertise to their own problems. Although information itself may change, the understanding of its management and use is fundamental to everyone.

Isolated and unco-ordinated pockets of skills and practice in this field have been identified in the past few years (although none of them are inherently 'new') but they have tended to be used and seen in isolation. For example, it was not considered illogical to teach a student how to use the Encyclopaedia Britannica in all its complicated glory, but not how to use a railway guide or find the address of his nearest Citizens Advice Bureau or youth clubs.

If there is an approach towards a total school or college learning skills policy, then some of these 'isolationist' problems can to a certain extent be overcome. This is difficult to achieve in many cases, as decisions have to be made which break down departmental and subject barriers, and so there are problems both in planning and effecting a learning to learn policy. Ideally such a policy should have its roots in the infant school, develop at the junior level, and achieve fruition at secondary school, so that the pupil or student can go on to further and higher education or work, equipped to cope with learning at all levels, and particularly able to cope with his or her individual information needs. All too often these skills are now tacked on to social and life skills courses, when their relevance is more difficult for the student to understand.

In the majority of cases any learning to learn programme and its details will be determined to some extent by the inevitable constraints of examination structures, funding, curricular constraints and LEA support. Student motivation, attitudes, styles of learning and previous experiences must also be considered. The policy and process should determine content, and not vice versa, or the student will be artificially constrained. It may be helpful to compile a 'map' showing the sub skills needed within each broad skill area, such as the skills inherent in reading proficiency for example, and how these could and do relate to subject departments within the school, including the library. If, as part of this exercise, any core elements can be isolated, such as alphabetisation, these could form part of a central package and be taught in conjunction with specialist subject departments. Very specific and subject based skills, isolated as discrete elements and not forming part of the central package, could then be integrated into the relevant subject areas. This 'map' could then be built up year by year until it can be integrated into the complex information skills techniques which are taught at fifth and sixth form levels, and which should reinforce the basic skills taught and practised earlier, as part of the building up of skills exercises.

In many cases the ubiquitous and universal project is the vehicle which can be used to ensure that students have acquired basic skills, and that they can plan, find, use, present and evaluate the information finding process, which is at the core of this activity. Before any project can be planned in detail, it is essential to determine what skills a student needs to acquire in relation to carrying out any project, what he needs for a particular or specific project and, finally, what skill or range of skills the project hopes to develop. This pre-planning then ensures that the skills mentioned above are relevant, relate to student needs, and do not include unrealistic aims or skills.

Planning and defining problems

If the project is to be used as a vehicle then the primary task is its planning, by both pupils and teachers. The aims and objectives relating to the department, the resources, time and staff available and the learning needs of the pupils, including the defining of what skills and knowledge will be involved and needed, have to be defined. These will include the essential skills, but lead on to others that will enable the pupil to cope with life outside school. There are many definitions of these social and life skills, but they include the ability to adapt, to anticipate answers and respond to them, to be aware of and formulate a problem, to construct and implement a strategy, to gather information, and be able to communicate. The summary of an information skills curriculum quoted in the Schools Council Curriculum Bulletin 9 (Schools Council 1981) provides the essential planning framework. Helping individual pupils to formulate and plan their projects is the primary objective at this stage, and this can be achieved through a variety of activities, including the use of topic webs, discussion, browsing in the library, checking reference books, looking for a definition of terminology in the dictionary, identifying key words in the problem area,

resources for learning: an outline map of learning skills

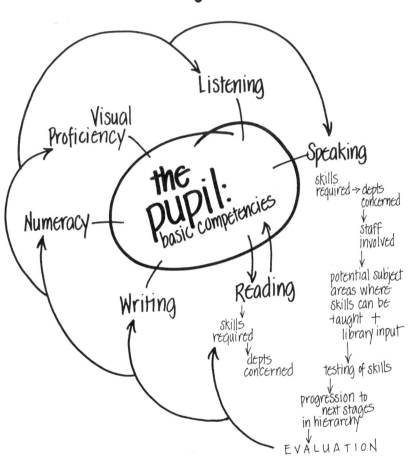

the pupil: basic competencies

Visual Proficiency

Listening

Speaking

Numeracy

Writing

Reading

skills required → depts concerned

staff involved

potential subject areas where skills can be taught + library input

testing of skills

progression to next stages in hierarchy

skills required

depts concerned

EVALUATION

composing a grid, or a combination of these. The pupil or student is at this stage learning to organise himself, set himself time or subject limits, and

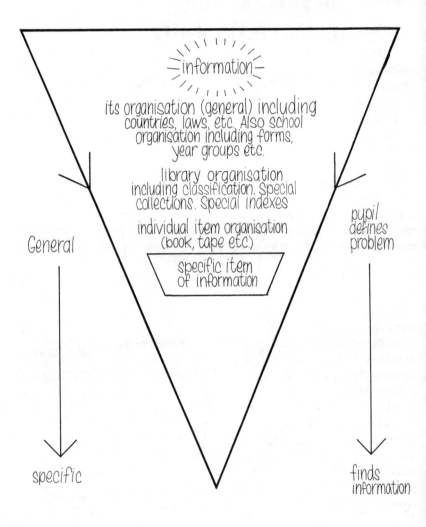

generally begin to work towards autonomy. If at any of the planning stages it is possible for the librarian or teacher to define the parameters and strategies involved in an information skills programme, this can be very helpful. It should include the title of the course or programme, the aim and objectives, the content, learning strategies, teaching methods, media, assessment and evaluation.

Finding information through understanding how and why it is organised is the next logical step in this process.

Finding information

Defining the parameters of a topic or problem is logically followed by isolating areas, places and people where information on the topic can be obtained, including the library resource centre (hence the importance of good relevant publicity and guidance). Ensure that both publicity materials and guidance on the library use simple language. Confusing terminology and jargon will just lead to lack of use of the library and erect yet another barrier for the student. Finding the library and finding his or her way around it involves the librarian in being familiar with pupil and student levels of expertise, their language proficiency (guiding may be necessary in more than one language), and their expectations. As in all other areas of planning, note must be taken of the study modes of pupils and teachers, and the differences in teaching and learning styles. This enables the librarian to relate his or her ways of helping students find information to other styles of activity in the school.

The next logical stage is coping with the organisation of the information once it has been located. An explanation of the philosophy and organisation of information and resources could be linked to a contribution from the class teacher, using examples within the school, such as the organisation of forms, houses, pastoral care groups, age and geographical divisions. This can then lead into an input from the librarian on the basic thinking behind classification and bibliographical control, so that the concept of planned organisation and control, as part of the process of locating information, becomes very clear. This can then enable the librarian to explain the organisation of individual items and the organisation of special collections of materials, such as reference books, and can illustrate ways of pinpointing specific information. If this standard procedure of working from the general to the specific is planned as part of a personal problem, and is illustrated in context, it has meaning for the pupil, and also enables the librarian and teacher to work as a team, supporting the pupil.

Managing and using information

Having identified and located a particular item, the student then needs to be able to use the materials, regardless of format, either to enrich his own personal needs, or to extract information as part of a problem solving exercise. Being able to manage and use resources includes the ability to make personal decisions, to make organisational decisions and to record relevant information. In order to do this he or she must possess the skills necessary to extract and record information, including reading, skimming, scanning, notetaking, drawing, interpreting diagrams, watching and discussing. If materials in all formats are available for use, then the pupil must also be able to cope with any necessary equipment, and so there is also a need for physical dexterity. He or she must also be able to collect information or data from other sources, such as museums, people and ephemera. These activities involve the application of social skills. The skills involved stem from basic or core skills and are refinements or sub-sets of these core skills — listening, speaking, reading, writing, numeracy and visual literacy. It is also important that the pupil or student should have the necessary skills in evaluating material, including its currency, bias, quality, accuracy of the source used, review bias, the physical production and quality, and the reputation of the author or publisher. This is a very difficult area, but the point can be illustrated by illustrating inaccuracy or bias in a subject or hobby with which the student or teacher is very familiar. Pupils must learn to distinguish between facts which can be checked, and the personal opinions of an author or publisher, and be able to compare information taken from several sources and then evaluate it. They must also be aware of and able to assess the power of persuasive argument, as against fact, and not be influenced by their own opinions. These are all very sophisticated skills, and will take a considerable time to acquire. If a planning framework is maintained, then the extracting, evaluating and recording of information are all clearly part of its use and management. The sophisticated ability to use information to support an argument or to use a wide range of information to support several arguments or hypotheses, as in thesis writing, is the ultimate achievement. The synthesising of information is a skill about which many assumptions are made, but for which little guidance is given.

Presenting information

Once the required information has been extracted from a source or variety of sources, both formal and informal, then it can be organised, marshalled into a coherent pattern, and presented. The methods and style used will depend on whether the exercise is entirely for personal use, or part of a planned project which is aimed at integrating information skills into an area or areas of the curriculum. The extent and physical presentation will form part of the student's planning strategy, and information can be given as a written report, a verbal report, or tape or film can be used. It should include an indication of where the information has been found, so that a structure is maintained. The exercise should be intended to illustrate the sequential organisation of information, its extraction, recording, evaluation and consolidation, into some kind of evidence or report and synthesisation.

Evaluating information skills

The final process is that of evaluation, when all factors have to be considered by the pupils and teachers working on the project, in relation to the skills and expertise they have acquired. It is also necessary to assess what flaws and gaps are apparent, what changes could and should be made to the plan, and the implications for future curriculum planning. Pupils should be able to assess what conclusions they have reached personally as a result of acquiring new skills, strategies and information. They should be able to assess if this has changed any of their previously held personal ideas, and if they now feel more competent and able to repeat the exercise at other levels, both in a personal and in a curricular setting. Hopefully pupils may also be able to assess whether they are now personally more competent to deal with information, as part of their socialising skills. The librarian should use any feedback to assess the stock, services, and use of the library, and make the exercise contribute to an on-going evaluation and planning process. The teacher will be able to evaluate techniques and strategies and, again at both an individual and corporate level, feed back this information into school planning activities.

In addition to an involvement in the wide school and college policies concerned with learning skills it can sometimes be effective to teach older pupils how to carry out a standard search procedure. This is of course much narrower in concept, but is of value when preparing students for further education.

Standard search procedures

In general: work from general to specific and from recent to older materials.

1. Define topic and set units (time, size, length, date, etc.)

2. To do this use relevant search tools e.g. encyclopaedias, standard works on the subject, reference books — dictionaries, directories, manuals, biographical dictionaries, and abstracting and indexing journals.

3. From these make a list of sources to be consulted and checked (e.g. lists which could produce both books and materials). Note details

resources for learning: information skills

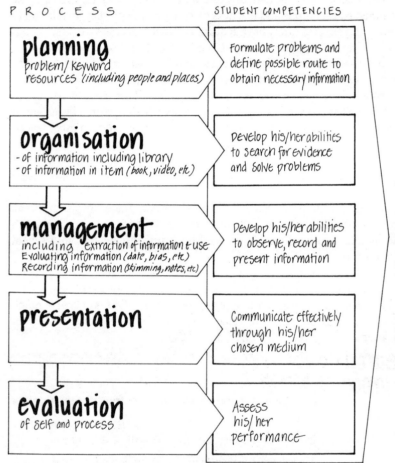

PROCESS

STUDENT COMPETENCIES

planning
problem / keyword
resources (including people and places)

Formulate problems and define possible route to obtain necessary information

organisation
- of information including library
- of information in item (book, video, etc.)

Develop his/her abilities to search for evidence and solve problems

management
including extraction of information & use
Evaluating information (date, bias, etc.)
Recording information (skimming, notes, etc.)

Develop his/her abilities to observe, record and present information

presentation

Communicate effectively through his/her chosen medium

evaluation
of self and process

Assess his/her performance

STUDENT AUTONOMY

of books. Note details of relevant bibliographies, for a) specific subjects b) local collections c) recent works on a national scale d) guides to the literature.

4. From these also make a list of search terms under which to look for information. Use imagination, but stick to pattern.

5. Start looking at books and materials in own and nearest available (relevant) library. Use catalogues efficiently. Record material and keep checks on references yet to be checked. Use national bibliographies to ensure a total check.

6. Then progress to the following sources for information:

Journals	Abstracts and indexes
Theses	Reports
Research	Parliamentary papers
Other specialist libraries	Materials in other formats (if organised separately).

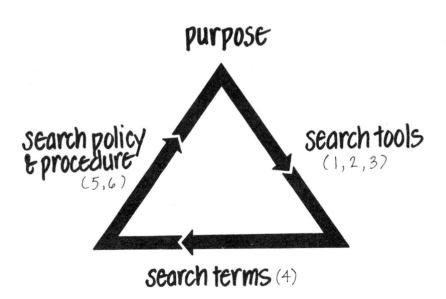

purpose

search policy & procedure (5,6)

search tools (1, 2, 3)

search terms (4)

Level 4 Extra-curricular activities (school based)

There are many informal ways of exploiting the library and of making its services known. Personality is of course one of them, and although this is a difficult area to pin down, it is essential for anyone concerned with this area of education to be outward looking and involved with people. It then becomes easier to run book clubs for pupils and students, involving as many members of staff as possible. Bookshops, book weeks (in co-operation with national organisations) and reviewing schemes are all effective ways of further exploiting the library. Other reading activities, such as story telling, reading linked to other activities, and festivals related to differing ethnic groups are rewarding. Links with the local public library are very fruitful, over holiday reading schemes for example, or with local Book Buses and other 'happenings'. Visiting speakers and lecturers can very effectively make sure that the community is well aware of its library and the resources there, and can use the library to illustrate the provision of materials for ethnic groups, or for demonstrating the importance of information and information handling as part of rapid technical innovations at a national level. Changes in authority policy and strategies at a local level can also be demonstrated through exploiting the library and linking it to other local services, such as culture activities, information centres and training initiatives.

Level 5 Extra-curricular activities (outside school or college)

Forming links with the local community as well as with the careers and counselling groups in colleges is, as mentioned earlier, of great value in further involving the resources of the library with as many groups of users as possible, and expanding the ways in which resources can be used. This can be through working with groups concerned with local history, civic amenities, legal rights or local publishers, in addition to local radio and television and community broadcasting. Radio programmes can support reading initiatives, such as the 'personal enrichment' of providing books which have been serialised, and also the provision of story books to support programmes of reading for young children. Libraries can act as focal points for giving out information, as in the *Roadshow* programmes produced by the BBC, and programmes such as *Speak for yourself*, and in considerable numbers of 'social action' programmes provided by local radio, aiming at support for the elderly, for young adults, and for those who need counselling advice. These advice services, covering careers, educational opportunities and learning skills, are growing fast, and many are using libraries as an initial information and referral point, leading into more detailed advice and guidance services. Their use and potential is a crucial opportunity for librarians, so that they are involved as information specialists, but can also become personally involved in new initiatives. Many queries on college courses and open learning result from initial queries in public libraries, and the considerable number of education guidance services in existence illustrates the need to use library resources at a local level more effectively. Local groups have local expertise, and the library should be at the core of such activities, so that national networks are utilised by local initiatives. Local coordinating committees can be organised, involving library staff, who can be actively involved in directing users on where and how to use resources, and not function as mere storehouses of information. Thus libraries can truly function as resource centres.

Conclusion

Curriculum development, as a result of changing expectations and ideas, is leading to a heightened awareness of an increased need to integrate changes into school and college policies. If pupils and students are to be able to cope with a rapidly changing environment, then their needs and expectations have to be re-considered. This involves a re-assessment of teaching methods and assessment, and of management techniques, related to the changes outlined in the first section. Pupils must leave school or college with the ability to define problem areas, extract information, synthesise information obtained from a variety of sources in relation to their problem, and solve problems (personal or otherwise) from the information collected or given. These skills are universal, and can be applied to a variety of situations and needs, ranging from the very simple to the complex. The process of planning for change, the reviewing to ensure that objectives have been achieved, ensures meaningful direction within a school or college.

resources for learning: planning levels

plan/activity	level	priority	involvement
Extra Curricular Activities (outside)	level 5	could	school and community
Extra Curricular Activities (school-based)	level 4	should	school-based activities
Learning to Learn — Policy & Strategies	level 3	must	student, teachers and librarian with management
Basic Use of Resources — Planning & Integration	level 2	must	student, teachers and librarian with management
Introduction Orientation e.g. physical arrangement	level 1	must	student, teachers and librarian

INFORMATION

● Information — a selective list of relevant groups, institutes and associations

British Broadcasting Corporation
(BBC)
Educational Liaison Offices
The Langham
London WC1A 44GS

BBC Computer Literacy Project
BBC Broadcasting Centre
Room 125
Woodhouse Lane
Leeds LS2 9PX

British Library Information Officer for
User Education
I. Malley
Loughborough University of
Technology
Loughborough
Leics. LE11 3TU

Careers Research and Advisory
Centre
Bateman Street
Cambridge

Centre for Mass Communication
Research
University of Leicester
University Road
Leicester
Leics. LE1 7RH

Centre for Research on User Studies
(CRUS)
University of Sheffield
Western Bank
Sheffield S10 2TN

Centre for the Study of Human
Learning
Brunel University
Uxbridge
Middx.

Clocktower Project
The Clocktower
Tower Road North
Warmley
Bristol BS15 2XL

Community Information Project
Library Association
7 Ridgmount Street
London WC1E 7AE

Developing Information Concepts
and Skills: instructional materials
Ms. A. Irving
Department of Library & Information
Studies
Loughborough University
Loughborough
Leics.

Education for Neighbourhood
Change
School of Education
Nottingham University
Nottingham NG7 2RD

Educational Advisory Services
Project
The Open University (Yorkshire
Region)
Fairfax House
Merrion Street
Leeds LS2 8JU

ERIC (Educational Resources
Information Center)
National Institute of Education
1200 19th St. NW
Washington DC 20208
USA

Federation of Children's Book
Groups
6 Cavendish Court
Park Road
Eccleshill
Bradford

Information Skills in the Curriculum
Research Unit (INSCRU)
Centre for Learning Resources
275 Kennington Lane
Vauxhall SE11 5QZ

Information Use and Learning Styles
E. Martin
Centre for Educational Research and
Development
Cartmel College
Bailrigg,
Lancaster

Learning Styles of Young People
Post-16 Project
(Further Education Unit)
Industrial Training Research Unit Ltd
Cambridge

Library Access, Library Use and User
Education in Academic Sixth Forms
CARE
University of East Anglia
Norwich

Link between Library User Education
in Schools and Library Use in Tertiary
Education
Jim Stephenson
Faculty of Humanities
Newcastle upon Tyne Polytechnic
Newcastle

Materials for 11-14 year-old students
to assist them to become better users
of information
Brian Lake
Romsey School
Romsey
Hants

A microcomputer emulation of online
bibliographic searching
Dr J.A. Large
College of Librarianship Wales
Llanbadarn Fawr
Aberystwyth
Dyfed

National Book League
The Book House
45 East Hill
Wandsworth
London SW18 2QZ

National Youth Bureau
17-23 Albion Street
Leicester LE1 6GD

Reading for Learning in the
Secondary School
Professor E.A. Lunzer and Keith
Gardner
School of Education
Nottingham University
Nottingham

The role of The School Librarian in
the curriculum
Margaret Ingram
Margaret Dane School
Bishops Stortford
Herts.

Schools Broadcasting Council
The Langham
Portland Place
London W1A 1AA

Schools Information Retrieval
Project (SIR)
Aslib
3 Belgrave Square
London SW1X 8PL

Sixth Form Studies and
Individualised Learning
Robin Hardwick
Council for Educational Technology
3 Devonshire Street
London WIN 2BA

Study Skills and Habits of Students
on A-level Courses, with particular
reference to their capacity for
independent work
Colin Swatridge
School of Education
Nottingham University
Nottingham

The supported self-study project
Philip Waterhouse
Council for Educational Technology
3 Devonshire Street
London W1N 2BA

Teaching of Study Skills Project
NFER
Upton House
The Mere
Slough
Berks

Training material in the use of Prestel
T. Wood
Dept. of Library and Information
Studies
Manchester Polytechnic
Manchester

United Kingdom Reading Association
c/o Edge Hill College of Higher
Education
St. Helen's Road
Ormskirk
Lancs

Using Books and Libraries Project
D. Hounsell
Centre for Educational Research and
Development
Cartmel College
Bailrigg
Lancaster

Volunteer Reading Help (Capital
Radio)
c/o Centre for Language in Primary
Education (ILEA)
Sutherland Street
London SW1V 4LH

● Journals — a selective list

Aslib Information
Aslib
3 Belgrave Square
London SW1X 8PL

Audiovisual Librarian
Periodical Subscriptions
Aslib
3 Belgrave Square
London SW1X 8PL

CET News
Council for Educational Technology
3 Devonshire Street
London W1N 2BA

CRUS News
Centre for Research on User Studies
University of Sheffield
Western Bank
Sheffield S10 2TN

Education Libraries Bulletin
University of London
Institute of Education Library
11-13 Ridgmount Street
London WC1E 7AH

Information Design Journal
R. Waller
P.O. Box 185
Milton Keynes
MK7 6BL

Infuse
I. Malley
British Library Information Officer for
User Education
Loughborough University of
Technology
Loughborough
Leics. LE11 3TU

ISG News
Newsletter of the SCONUL Advisory
Committee on Information Service
The Library
University of Leicester
University Road
Leics. LE1 7RH

*Library and Information Research
News*
c/o Alan Cooper
Department of Library and
Information Studies
Loughborough University
Loughborough
Leics. LE11 3TU

*Library and Information Science
Abstracts (LISA)*
Library Association
7 Ridgmount Street
London WC1E 7AE

LOEX News (Library Orientation
Exchange)
Eastern Michigan University
Ypsilanti
Michigan 48197
USA

Media Project News
The Volunteer Centre
29 Lower Kings Road
Berkhamsted
Herts. HP4 2AB

Study Skills Newsletter
Teaching of Study Skills Project
NFER
The Mere
Upton Park
Slough
Bucks.

● **References — a selective list of relevant books, reports and articles**

Advisory Centre for Adult and Continuing Education. *Directory of Educational Guidance Services for Adults.* Leicester, ACACE, 1981.
The Audio Visual Club. London, CET, 1975. (Film) (Media and methods case study no. 2).
Beeler, R. J. *Evaluating library use instruction.* Ann Arbor, Mich., Pierian Press, 1975.

Beswick, B. *Producing lists of learning resources.* London, CET, 1979 (Guidelines 7).

Biggs, J. R. *Basic typography.* London, Faber & Faber, 1968.

Brake, T. 'Educating for access into the information culture' in *Education Libraries Bulletin.* 23.2.(68), Summer 1980, pp. 1-14.

Brewer, J. G. and Hills, P. J. 'Evaluation of reader instruction' in *Libri,* 26(1), 1976, pp. 55-65.

British Library. *Review Committee on Education for Information Use. Final report.* London, British Library, 1977. (Research and Development Report 5325).

Buzan, T. *Use your head.* BBC, 1974.

Cabeceiras, J. *The multi media library: materials selection and use.* London, Academic Press, 1978.

Carey, R. J. P. *Library guiding. A programme for exploiting library resources.* London, Bingley, 1974.

Carey, R. J. P. 'Making libraries easy to use: a systems approach' in *Library Association Record,* 73, 1971, pp. 132-135.

Clark, D. *Students and Libraries.* Newcastle, Polytechnic Products Ltd, 1981.

Craig, J. *Designing with type.* London, Pitman, 1980.

Cronin, B. *A national graphics resource centre for libraries in the United Kingdom.* London, Aslib, 1981.

Current R. & D. projects in user education in the UK 1980. Papers of the Second Annual Conference held at Loughborough University by the Library and Information Research Group (LIRG). Edited by Ian Malley, Loughborough, British Library Information Officer for User Education, 1980.

Dair, C. *Design with type.* Toronto, University of Toronto Press, 1967.

Davies, R. A. *School library media program: instruction force for excellence.* New York, Bowker, 2nd ed, 1979.

De Bono, E. *Teaching thinking.* London, Temple Smith, 1976.

Department of Education and Science. *A language for life.* London, HMSO, 1975 (The Bullock Report).

Dudley, M. *Library resources: a self-directed course in the use of UCLA's college library.* Los Angeles, University of California, College Library, 1979.

Evans, A. J., Rhodes, R. G. and Keenan, S. *Education and training of users of scientific and technical information.* UNISIST guide for teachers. Unesco, 1977.

Fenner, P. and Armstrong, M. C. *Research: a practical guide to finding information.* Los Altos, Wilhem Kaufman, 1982.

Fjallbrant, N. 'Teaching methods for the education of the library user' in *Libri,* 26(4), 1976, pp. 252-267.

Ford, G. *User studies: an introductory guide and select bibliography.* Sheffield, CRUS, University of Sheffield, 1977.

Freeman, R. *How to study effectively.* Cambridge, National Extension College,

1972.

Garland, K. *Graphics glossary.* London, Barrie & Jenkins, 1980.

Garland, K. *Graphics handbook.* London, Studio Vista, 1966 (out of print).

Gibbs, G. *Learning to study: a guide to running group sessions.* Milton Keynes, Open University, 1977.

Gibbs, G. *Teaching students to learn.* Milton Keynes, Open University, 1966.

Hamblin, D. *Teaching study skills.* Oxford, Blackwell, 1981.

Hamblin, D. *The teacher and pastoral care.* Oxford, Blackwell, 1978.

Harris, C. *Illuminative evaluation of user education programmes* in Aslib Proceedings, 29(10), October 1977, pp. 348-62.

Hart, T.L. (ed.) *Instruction in school media centre use.* Chicago, American Library Association, 1978.

Herring, J. E. *Teaching library skills in schools.* Windsor, NFER, 1978.

Hills, P. J. 'Library instruction and the development of the individual' in *Journal of Librarianship,* 6(4), 1974, pp. 255-63.

Hills, P. J. *Study courses and counselling: problems and possibilities.* Guildford, Society for Research into Higher Education, 1979.

Hills, P. J. *The future of the printed word.* London, Pinter, 1980.

Hounsell, D., Martin E., Needham, G. and Jones, H. *Educational information and the teacher.* London, British Library, 1980. (Research and Development Report 5505).

Information skills in the secondary school curriculum. London, Methuen Educational, 1981 (Schools Council Curriculum Bulletin 9).

Ireland, R.J. *Producing guides to local resources.* London, CET, 1979 (Guidelines 6).

Irving, A. (ed.) *Starting to teach study skills.* Maidenhead, Arnold, 1982.

Irving, A. and Snape, W. H. *Educating library users in secondary schools.* London British Library, 1979 (Research and Development Report 5467).

Kirk, T. 'Bibliographic instruction — a review of research' in Richard Beeler, Jr. (ed.) *Evaluating library use instruction.* Ann Arbor, Michigan, Pierian Press, 1975, pp. 1-29.

Knapp, P. B. 'The meaning of the Monteith Program for Library Education' in *Journal of Education for Librarianship 6,* Fall, 1965, pp. 117-27.

Kobelski, P. and Reichel, M. 'Conceptual frameworks for bibliographic instruction' in *Journal of Academic Librarianship,* 7, May 1981, pp. 73-77.

Lindsay, J. 'Information training in secondary schools' in *Education Libraries Bulletin,* 19(3), 1976, pp. 16-21.

Lockwood, D. L., (comp.) *Library instruction: a bibliography.* Westport, Conn, Greenwood Press, 1979.

Lubans, J. *Educating the library user.* London, New York, Bowker, 1974.

Lubans, J. *Progress in educating the library user.* London, New York, Bowker, 1978.

Lunzer, E. and Gardner, K. *The effective use of reading.* London, Heinemann

Educational Books for the Schools Council, 1979.

Main, A. *Encouraging effective learning.* Edinburgh, Scottish Academic Press, 1980.

Malley, I. *Evaluation in user education: an annotated bibliography.* Loughborough, INFUSE Publications, 1982.

Malley, I. *User education in polytechnics and colleges: an annotated bibliography.* Loughborough, INFUSE Publications, 1982.

Malley, I. *User education in schools: an annotated bibliography.* Loughborough, INFUSE publications, 1982.

Malley, I. and Fjallbrant, N. *User education in libraries.* London, Bingley, 1983.

Marland, M., *Language across the curriculum.* London, Heinemann Educational Books, 1977.

Open University. *Preparing to study.* Milton Keynes, Open University, 1979.

Parlett, M. and Hamilton, D. *Illuminative evaluation.* Edinburgh, University of Edinburgh, Centre for Research in Educational Sciences, 1976 (Occasional paper 9).

Pollet, D. and Haskell, P. *Sign systems for libraries.* London, New York, Bowker, 1979.

Reynolds, L. and Barnett, S. *Signs and guiding for libraries.* London, Bingley, 1981.

Rowntree, D. *Learn how to study.* London, Macdonald, 1970.

Smith, J. M. and Winkworth, F. V. *A bibliography of teaching materials for schools and colleges of further education.* London, British Library, 1978.

Social Action and the media. Berkhamsted, The Volunteer Centre, 1980.

Spencer, H. and Reynolds, L. *Directional signing and labelling in libraries and museums: a review of current theory and practice.* London Royal College of Art, Readability of Print Research Unit, 1977.

Stevenson, M. B. *User education programmes: a study of their development, organization, methods and assessment.* Boston Spa, British Library, Research Reports, 1977.

Sullivan, T. *Grammar.* Cambridge, National Extension College, 1979 (Studying Skills series).

Sullivan, T. *Reading and understanding.* Cambridge, National Extension College, 1979 (Studying Skills series).

Sullivan, T. *Studying.* Cambridge, National Extension College, 1979 (Studying Skills series).

Sullivan, T. *Writing.* Cambridge, National Extension College, 1979 (Studying Skills series).

Tabberer, R. and Allman, J. *Study skills at 16 plus.* Windsor, NFER, 1981 (NFER Research in Progress 4).

Taylor, P. J. *Information guides: a survey of subject guides to sources of information produced by library and information services in the United Kingdom.* London, British Library, Research and Development Department

(British Library Research and Development Report 5440).

Travelling workshops experiment in library user education. London, British Library, 1982 (British Library Research and Development Report 5602).

University of Lancaster Centre for Educational Research and Development. *Information skills in secondary school and teaching resource folder.* Lancaster, Using Books and Libraries Project, University of Lancaster, 1980.

Usherwood, R. *The visible library.* London, Library Association, 1981.

Vernon, T. *Gobbledegook.* London, National Consumer Council, 1980.

Vincent, K. *A survey of the methods by which teachers select books.* Sheffield, Centre for Research on User Studies, University of of Sheffield, 1980 (CRUS occasional paper 3).

Werking, R.H. 'Evaluating bibliographic education: a review and critique' in *Library Trends 29* Summer 1980, pp. 153-172.

White, J.V. *Editing by design.* London, New York, Bowker, 1974.

Winkworth, F. *User education in schools: a survey of the literature on education for library and information use in schools.* London, British Library, 1977. (Research and Development Report 5391).

Planning pointers

- Be informed about the ways in which pupils learn, and plan the ways in which the library can contribute to these processes.

- Be involved in any school learning to learn policy. Join any related groups or committees and contribute to their thinking.

- Plan any library programmes to relate and support these policies.

- Work out the stages in the strategic planning of such programmes, in cooperation with subject teachers and pupils. Check that resources are available and organised.

- Validate any programmes.

- Evaluate any programmes and replan as necessary.

11 Staffing resources: in-service training and staff development

Introduction

In-service training and staff development exist at all levels and in some form in most libraries, and their value is universally acknowledged. Activities range from in-house orientation and induction activities and support from advisers and specialist centres, to large scale personnel exercises at local authority level. These represent the macro level (the authority) and the micro level (the school).

Although many school libraries do not have any ancillary help, some are lucky enough to have both professional and non-professional support. Situations do change, and in any case successful in-service training and staff development systems maximise expertise available, and so are crucial to management planning, in both larger and smaller libraries. It is helpful to have an understanding of the place of training and development within an institution, as this contributes to any long-term planning activities. Once the principle has been established then detailed programmes can be worked out later as the initial planning is the crucial element.' This can be seen now to be particularly important in the area of the new technology, which has training and development implications for the management of change (organisational structures, their planning and information needs); for training in new techniques (implications of the system); and for the training and development of staff attitudes (personnel involvement, reactions and training).

At all levels and with all new developments systems will not support users if the staffing implications are neglected or under emphasised. The implications of the new technology relate to information and information skills and the handling of these skills, so that librarians must contribute to this environment of information change, so that their subject knowledge and information handling knowledge both contribute to and support the institutional needs.

Training and development

Training can be defined as a discipline and institution directed to development of powers of formation of character, education, systematic instruction and exercise in some art, profession or occupation, with a view to proficiency in it, whereas development can be defined as a gradual unfolding; a fuller working out of the details of a policy.

Training and development are linked and complementary activities, as are the philosophies behind them. To a certain extent both are determined by national changes at a very wide level, such as social and economic trends, which in turn influence educational and professional developments. More specific changes, such as curriculum content and organisation, new technology, and the administrative structures which organise services, also determine policies and strategies. Major reports indicating national trends and changes also have a direct or indirect effect on training. For example the James Report affected the training of teachers, as did the Heycocks Report, and libraries and librarians have in turn to respond to new educational needs. In general, in-service training is considered to be specifically related to a task or post, and is an enabling and training process which allows a librarian or other members of staff to carry out this task more effectively. It usually includes at the initial stages the orientation and induction of new staff to their places of work and to the library services and then leads into the more job-specific training area. This relationship of training to a particular job or area of development is also influenced strongly by the national changes outlined earlier.

Staff development is more closely related to the personal career development and professional enrichment of the individual, and his or her other personal aspirations over a period of time. Development involves identifying potential areas of need and supplying activities and information to further job satisfaction, adding to both career prospects and to personal enrichment. Both activities are inherently part of the wider aims of the total library service, and the aims and philosophies of the individual school. This inter-relationship has to exist to make any staffing and development policies have real significance.

Both in-service training and staff development can possibly be isolated into three categories of perception. The identification of these three categories can help in planning, so that overlap and duplication can be avoided.

The first category is that which is universal or common, e.g. most authorities and establishments acknowledge the need for, and provide some kind of staff training and development. Both activities can be seen to lead to better performances, to be cost effective, to give increased job satisfaction, and to improve the effectiveness of library services in terms of plant, people and materials. Establishments also benefit, as people respond to changes in consumer needs. An increase in development possibilities and development is linked to an improvement in performance — this is a core element in both training and staff development, and is easily seen and acknowledged.

Secondly, many ideas and trends are common to the aims, objectives and needs of most institutions, and these can be called mainstream ideas. They often include activities centred on basic areas of educational provision, such as the organisation, management or exploitation of resources. These activities can in turn lead on to further developmental ideas, involving people, current practice and policy developments within the institution, so that these core concepts are supported through further initiatives.

Some ideas and needs are however specific to particular places and to local perception of needs, and these represent the third category of activity. Most activities here are those which are involved with the local process or orientation and induction ('scene setting'), and with supporting and developing particular services related to a particular community.

The problems of the inner city, of multi-cultural library provision, of scattered rural populations, community libraries or areas with identifiable ethno-cultural groups are examples of very localised needs, which will influence training and development activities.

Training and development can also be seen to operate at several levels, and these can be defined under the following headings:

Task specific

In-service training relating to a particular task must link both with the job description, and what is demanded of a particular person. Skills and operations cannot be demanded if the training is not and has not been provided. Questions to be asked when planning this kind of training are why? what? when? by whom? How will it be validated? How will it be evaluated? Is it more effective if it is related to real problems? It aims at professional competency at two levels: in the context of librarianship, and in the context of the college/LEA service in its social environment.

Development of the individual

This is, as illustrated earlier, a wider concept of initial training, and helps to build up personal development in relation to the expertise, career ambitions, and personal expectations of the individual. When planning any staff development programme this must reflect the philosophies and aims of the establishment so that programmes provide support for these.

201

Institutional development

Support for the institution is provided through activities at task specific and developmental levels. By integration of the individual, the library team and the school or college, each supports and stimulates the other (as in a whole school policy concerned with the development of learning skills for example).

All these levels are held together by the planning of training and development, determined by the changes indicated, and by the process (action), of what is actually achieved to carry out the aims. These are the programmes.

If the connected activities of planning, training and development, plus the process of providing programmes, link the individual, the team and the school, then it is important to consider the planning requirements inherent in these tasks, so that a framework for action is established, and a logical approach is developed.

Stage 1 — Planning

The stages to be considered can be identified as follows:

Establish objectives

These must relate to national changes, as indicated earlier, and to the structure within which the library functions. Objectives can be modest but must be clear.

Identify priorities and areas of need (e.g. what training and, for what purpose)

This involves identifying factors which are encouraging and forcing change, as these will probably be priorities. Some may be concerned with *curricular content* (e.g. TEC, BEC, C & G, MSC, UVP).

Others may be concerned with *curricular organisation*, e.g. open learning, flexistudy, recurrent education, continuing education.

There may also be changes in *user groups*. These will increasingly include ethnic minorities, women, mature students, part-time students, those on courses and training programmes for the long-term unemployed, and those obtaining industrial experience. Services will have to adapt to the needs of these users.

Also *social, political* and *economic* changes will need to be reflected by library stocks. Local environmental and political information should be available, and materials on counselling, mother tongue collections, industrial information and careers information should be considered.

Technical changes, including the development of computerised data bases, the increasing use of CAL, CAT, CAI, bibliographical control, and automatic document transmission also affect library services.

Factors which create motivation need to be identified and considered. These are important as development is linked to performance and performance is affected by motivation.

Many of these areas of need indicate a need for skills in working with committees, promoting the role of the librarian, designing materials, production and management, information on the cultures of minority groups, and all of these are potential training and development areas. The implications of manpower planning as well as personal and environmental effects must also be taken into account by the manager. These include both the psychological strain and physical strain of using some of the new technical aids, such as VDUs, and the social implications of changes in perceived and actual roles, work and professional development.

Identify the co-ordinating agents

This can be done through asking relevant questions, including:

Who will have overall responsibility for co-ordination? Who has the commitment to carry out the task?

Who will be involved — what staff? What library staff and teaching staff will participate in training and actually carry it out?

What exists already? How good is it? How much money is there?

Who is the target audience/receiver? Which members of staff will actually receive training?

What is the product and who will be involved in using the end result? (Consider film, video, etc., and what technical help is necessary.)

Stage 2 — Provision and organisation

This leads to the process/action, i.e. the provision of programmes, and the organisation of training.

The organisation of the actual training maintains the balance between the process and the action. The process involves setting up a method of planning, assessment and provision, leading to the construction of a policy. The action involves the organisation of a programme and actually providing the training. The planning phases of Stage 2 can also be identified and include the following:

Determine the objectives of the school/college.	These provide the framework of the provision.
Determine the objectives of the training programme.	These must derive from the wider objectives above.
Determine the priorities of the programme.	The areas of priority will be determined by the questions asked in the second *planning* stages.
Who will co-ordinate the programme?	The level and amount of staff involvement will be answered by the questions asked at the third planning stage.

Stage 3 — Training and strategies

It is now possible to identify what training and what strategies are to be used.

The identification of the question should help identify a possible solution, if a systematic approach has been taken.

What training
(relates to plans and policies)

Main areas

Orientation — sets of in-service activities and expectations. Introduces local scene and group level acceptance. Introduction to people and system, plus details of salaries, lunches, unions, health and safety, etc.

Induction — to the library services. Systematic introduction to the system. Includes introduction to people, such as the principal, and information on the service. Also the ethos and expectations of the service, plus the role of the librarian as communicator, e.g. verbal and non verbal communication, attitudes, dealing with complaints. Also to include visits to key areas of the service, to help perceive the system in total, and to think about possible career developments.

On-going training — as identified. Task specific.

On-going developments. As needed, developments related to personal needs. Also related to change factors.

When
(relates to activities)

Orientation. — First day. Induction — as soon as possible after joining service. On-going training and development — related to change factors.

Who

Clerical helpers. Ancillary helpers. Library assistant. Voluntary helpers, if possible. Also induction of new school and college teaching staff. Also participation in development programmes of senior teaching staff. This leads back to the provision, management and exploitation of resources, including people, and so illustrates the total integration and involvement of the library in training and development at all levels within the institution.

By whom

Depends on the objectives and priorities identified. Can include line managers, professional colleagues, training officers, outside experts, Library Association, Aslib, etc. Relates to costs, size of system and flexibility.

How

Centre-periphery model, or school or college based? Depends on local support and expertise available.

Training can include: check lists, booklets, diaries, job descriptions, talks/ seminars, packs, role play, case studies, simulation and games, visits, films, (note: choice of media relates to learning styles and teaching strategy and training methods).

Levels relate to professional needs and organisation needs.

Development can include: job rotation, exchange of staff, seminars, courses, local co-operative schemes, LEA support agencies, LEA expertise, Inspectors. Further professional study.

Validation

This is linked to the methods of course planning, so that it is possible to check if learning has taken place.

Feedback can include the use of: questionnaires (for quick check), interviews, observation, testing of skills (e.g. pre-and post-tests), annual interviews, achievement of stated objectives, diaries and training booklets,

There are various level of validation, at both personal and organisational levels. Questions to be asked relate to:

Has the organisation gained?

Has efficiency/output of the person (or dept.) improved?

Has learning been achieved?

What reaction can be observed as a result of training?

Interviews held with any staff who are resigning are also useful forms of validation for training and development programmes ('exit' interviews).

Overall there is a need for co-operation between the trainer, the trainee and the line manager, and there must be mutual trust between all these people involved.

Evaluation

This is a long-term process concerned with the effects of training and development in relation to an assessment of the institution as a whole, and is very difficult to carry out as so many educational and social issues are involved.

Evaluation can be achieved to a limited extent by senior staff carrying out a review of the service and checking to see if the objectives have been achieved, and also by carrying out an assessment of individual members of staff. Institutional assessment can be carried out on a departmental and personal basis, co-ordinated by the head or principal.

Self assessment can be carried out in a limited way through the use of check lists, completed by each individual, but in all cases both the person and the institution must be able and willing to be assessed. Evaluation is not the same as accountability, which is concerned with the effectiveness of institutions in relation to their funding and organisation in both the local authority and educational contexts.

In any training and development programme there is a need for both communication and collaboration. Communication should include the provision of policy statements, plans, details of proposed actions and details of programmes issued, if possible, through a staff development committee. (A wide involvement of staff in such committees ensures that everyone in the institution is aware of the professional function of the librarian and this is an added impetus.) Collaboration involves working with everyone concerned in an educational context, rather than in an isolated training context.

Research is needed in this whole area relating to factors such as costs, effectiveness, the effects of local initiatives, the effectiveness of validation programmes, and personal assessment programmes. The literature tends to be concerned with development and processes, rather than with the long-term training needs of education.

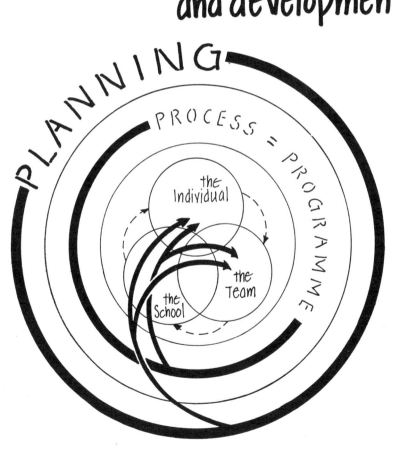

● Information — a selective list of relevant groups, institutes and associations

British Association for Commercial &
Industrial Education
16 Park Crescent
London W1N 4AP

British Industrial & Scientific Film
Association
26 D'Arblay Street
London W1V 3FH

Computers in Training as a Resource
Imperial College Computer Centre
Mechanical Engineering Building
Exhibition Road
London SW7 2BX

Council for Educational Technology
3 Devonshire Street
London W1N 2BA

Council for the Study of Management
Learning
School of Management and
Organisational Sciences
University of Lancaster
Lancaster LA1 4YX

Employment Relations Ltd
(incorporating the Industrial
Relations Training Resource Centre)
62 Hills Road
Cambridge CB2 1LA

Industrial Society
P.O. Box IBQ
Robert Hyde House,
Bryanston Square
London W1H 1BQ

Institute of Personnel Management
IPM House
Camp Road
Wimbledon
London SW19 4UW

Library Association
Sub-Committee on Training
7 Ridgmount Street
London WC1E 7AE

Local Government Training Board
The Arndale Centre
Luton
Beds.

Manpower Services Commission
(Training Services Division)
Selkirk House
High Holborn
London WC1V 6PF

National Association for Staff
Development in Further and Higher
Education
Redgrave House
Prestbury
Macclesfield
Cheshire

National Audio Visual Aids Centre
Paxton Place
Gipsy Road
London SE27 9SR

Training and Education Group
The Library Association
7 Ridgmount Street
London WC1E 7AE

Work Research Unit
Almack House
26 King Street
London SW1Y 6RB

● Journals — a selective list

Bacie Journal
British Association for Commercial
and Industrial Education
16 Park Crescent
London W1N 4AP

Training Newsletter
Local Government Training Board
Arndale Centre
Luton
Beds.

TEG Bulletin
Training and Education Group
The Library Association
7 Ridgmount Street
London WC1E 7AE

Training Officer
Marylebone Press Limited
25 Cross Street
Manchester M2 1WL

Training
(Institute of Training and
Development)
Pitman Periodicals Limited
41 Parker Street
London WC2

● References — a selective list of relevant books, reports and articles

Anderson, U. *Management training for librarians: a report.* London, Library Association, 1977.

Casteleyn, M. *Planning training programmes.* London, Deutsch, 1981.

Edwards, R. J. *In-service training in British Libraries.* London, Library Association, 1977.

George, D. *How to prepare for interviews: a practical guide.* London, Harrap, 1981.

Hackett, P. *Interview skills training: practice packs for trainers.* London, Institute of Personnel Management, 1981.

Library Association. Sub-Committee on training. *Guidelines for training in libraries.* London, Library Association, 1980.

Manpower Services Commission. *Training the trainers.* London, Manpower Services Commission, Training Services Division, 1981.

Savage, A. W. *Personnel management.* London, Library Association, 1977 (Library Association management pamphlet no. 1).

Tunley, M. *Library structures and staffing systems.* London, Library Association, 1979 (Library Association management pamphlet no. 2).

Vidal-Hall, J. *A guide to report writing.* London, Industrial Society, 1977.

Work Research Unit. *Introducing new technology into the office: a bibliography.* London, Work Research Unit, 1981.

Zachert, M. J. K. *Simulation teaching of library administration.* London, Bowker, 1975.

Planning pointers

- Find out what in-service training and staff development activities and facilities are available in (a) your school or college and (b) your LEA.

- Find out at what levels any current schemes operate.

- Decide what your planning objectives are for either your current staff or proposed (ideal) staffing structure. Also consider your own development needs.

- Work out a planning framework — stages 1, 2 and 3.

- Discuss validation and evaluation problems with those who will be providing the training (this may include you).

- Visit as many other establishments and institutions as possible and compare their provision and their planning with your own.

- Read some of the professional literature and translate the theories into practical librarianship training.

Part 4
OTHER CONSIDERATIONS

12   Evaluation

Evaluation is a facet of curriculum development which contributes to effective decision making and so to innovation and change. It is basically concerned with collecting and organising information (evidence) so that necessary decisions can be made. Although an emotive term, evaluation forms one element in the continuous process of planning, effecting planning, and deciding if the results reflect the aims of the original concepts. These concepts may relate to those who designed the curriculum, those who participated in it, and those involved in the wider educational context. This variety of involvement also adds to the complexity of the process. Frequently only the first phases in this cycle are carried out effectively, and the evaluation or evaluation processes are not given equal consideration. Although evaluation can take place during, as well as at the end of a project, it still remains a 'fringe' area. This may be partly because it is a complex process and is time consuming, and as it questions both ideas and assumptions, it is not a comfortable or comforting process. Evaluation is however essential to any form of curriculum planning and development, as from the results new ideas and processes are fed at some point into a new cycle of planning. Structures, teaching methods, teaching support, resources and staffing eventually reflect the results of evaluation. As evaluation is a long-term and intricate process, only a brief survey is attempted here and, unlike the situation in earlier years, the literature is now considerable. A review of this literature should be attempted by anyone who will be seriously involved in the area.

The process is complex partly because it is long term, partly because of the constant changes within education, partly because of the (sometimes) complex strategies and methodologies in use, and partly because of the inevitable gap between practitioner and researcher, which occurs in using some methodologies. Librarians need to build evaluation techniques into their planning. The methodology and models used (including identifying what the evaluation is for, who will do it, the formulation of a hypothesis, the choice of population, which materials are to be chosen, what methods used, what data allocated and what statistical techniques are to be used) are difficult and time consuming, but essential. The evaluation process is vital to both decision making and to innovation. Co-operation between the evaluator and other members of staff is essential, as the 'learning milieu' as a total picture has to be considered, as well as the role of the evaluator. The importance of the integration and use of resource materials within the

213

curriculum, the need for integrated professional support and development, and the planning of in-service activities must be apparent. The more extensive evaluation work that has been carried out within the context of user education has, in many cases, relied on an external evaluator, or evaluators, because of these problems, and because of the inherent problems of subjectivity. An outside evaluator can also relate to other research areas and other communities, and so help prevent an isolationist approach.

Crucial factors are the ability, as in any exercise of this sort, to know what questions to ask, when to ask them, and then to appreciate what techniques to use to support them, and what strategies to utilise. Sensitivity and responsiveness are two important qualities. It is however possible to isolate broadly and describe briefly some of the major approaches or strategies for evaluation which can be applied to the library context. It is important in this area not to assume broad ideas and apply them in simplistic ways, as both the carrying out of educational change and assessing the effectiveness of such changes are too complex to be seen as 'neat' systems, easily adopted. Much of this work in the educational field is still in the early stages, and librarianship has to some extent 'borrowed' from this discipline, which in turn relates to and draws from other sociological and anthropological areas.

Formative evaluation

This is a method of evaluation which tries to provide integral support for curriculum planning and methodology at all stages, so providing a constant and ongoing source of information and ideas during each phase of a programme. The information obtained is then re-cycled back into the course, so that either various parts or the whole can be modified. This is a methodology that involves the incorporating and understanding of the complex and localised relationships between both people and organisations involved in curriculum design and methodology. In essence it is descriptive rather than prescriptive. The evaluator has to be both skilled and flexible enough to apply techniques as and where he feels necessary, in relation to the perceived problems and in a variety of contexts with a variety of people.

Democratic evaluation

This method involves a wide approach, taking the school as a community, and using ideas and information from a wide variety of sources to contribute to decisions on curricula. In some ways this is very relevant to the area of librarianship in the educational context, because of the width of approach.

Summative evaluation

This method involves feeding information into the planning of the curriculum, so that decisions can be made on which final model should be adopted. Traditional research techniques are used, but problems arise over using these in conjunction with the more adaptable and 'open' curricula now available. The methodology should enable final decisions to be made on the effects and values of a programme and its future use.

Illuminative evaluation

This is one of the new approaches to evaluation, and was originally based on a paradigm designed for botanical research. It has developed into a more 'localised' approach with sociological roots, in which the evaluator is to a large extent dependent on people and situations in a more fixed context. The evaluator has to work within a given complicated situation while exploring the implications of that situation in relation to evaluation. A single technique or a variety of techniques may have to be used and another of the skills of the evaluator is deciding which is the most appropriate. No particular method or methods are used and it is the problem itself, in the context of the complicated learning network, which determines methodology.

. . . illuminative evaluation takes account of the wider contexts in which educational programmes function. Its primary concern is with description and interpretation rather than measurement and prediction. . . . In short it seeks to address and to illuminate a complex array of questions.

(Parlett, M. and Dearden, G. *Introduction to illuminative evaluation.* London, Society for Research into Higher Education, 1981.)

Evaluation also includes the area of pupil assessment, as part of the planning process. This relates both to pupil performance in traditional examinations, and in personal achievement. Assessment can be carried out in these traditional ways (the examination being the most well used and well known) and in other ways. These include the compilation of pupil profiles, continuous assessment, and others. Self-assessment (teacher based self-assessment) is another facet to be considered. Both are inherent parts of the wider issue of accountability. Schools, local authorities and elected members should be aware of and informed about current practices, so that there are increasingly responsible commitments and attitudes towards publicly financed activities and investments. The obligatory publishing of examination results at the secondary level is an indication of an understanding of the importance of information necessary to make decisions on educational provision. In the current climate of financial constraints, the responsibility of those involved in education becomes increasingly apparent, and so the methods used in evaluation are crucial. Policies are implemented as a result of such reports. Again there is a considerable literature developing on the openness and availability of school records and information, as part of this intent. Within this area some local initiatives are developing, including the pilot scheme of annual and quinquennial reviews within the ILEA, and school evaluation schemes in Cambridgeshire and Solihull. In 1983 the ILEA will also introduce a 'portfolio' system within its schools, and each pupil will leave school with an individual record of his or her achievements, including individual pupil profiles. Initiatives on course evaluation have also taken place in the university sector as well as in the college sector, and research has been carried out by the Society for Research into Higher Education.

In the field of librarianship evaluation is in its very early stages. It has been concerned mainly with the assessment of programmes and materials in the context of user education and, as such, with improving the programmes and ideas which are offered, with re-planning such programmes after having received such evidence, and then hopefully offering more effective programmes to students and staff. As in education, problems relate to the complexity of the area, to the difficulty of giving any kind of research a place in the hierarchy of a system, and to the questioning of assumptions, never a comfortable process. It also questions the whole complex process of 'learning to learn', and the best ways to achieve this, while much emphasis has been placed in previous years on the narrower concepts of the exercises labelled 'user education'. Although this broadening of horizons will not resolve the difficulties inherent in the choice of methodologies, it will help prevent some of the problems occurring as a result of the earlier and isolationist approach.

The field is difficult also not only because of its own intrinsic problems, methodologies and background, but also because of the relationships between library 'systems' and a parent 'system' which, in the case of education, is in itself in a constant state of change. Within one department, in this case the library, there are a variety of relationships, ideas, methods and materials, which cannot be taken out of context and examined in isolation. Many programmes and initiatives are also fluid (or possibly instinctive), and so rigid techniques are difficult to apply. The fluidity and responsiveness of such programmes to perceived need (on the part of librarians) can also include the element of evaluation, as the librarian assesses its success or otherwise through personal strategies. The Travelling Workshops Experiment, funded by the British Library, was one research initiative that was formally concerned with evaluation as well as with innovation, and influenced programmes in the further and high education sectors.

The other aspect of evaluation which relates to librarianship is concerned with research into library services, and with assessing the effectiveness of a system or part of a system. This could apply, for example, to the effectiveness of a photocopying service or abstracting service, in relation to the overall aims and objectives of the library, or to the needs of Open University students. This is an area of growing concern, as the ability to identify measurements of output and evaluate them, in a climate of decreasing resources, is becoming crucial.

As mentioned earlier, many methodologies have their roots in other disciplines, which makes it difficult to evaluate or assess services in isolation, and there is a need for them to relate to overall policies and objectives. As with other disciplines, it is essential to formulate objectives before any testing can be carried out to see if they have been achieved, and achieved effectively. If outputs are to be measured, then the objectives and their implementation must be clear cut and well defined, so that programmes can be monitored and evaluated, and results fed into the next cycle of planning.

If the effectiveness of services is to be measured, then another result should be this automatic setting up of clear-cut goals and objectives, and this procedure in itself helps to establish the library as an organised and decisive department within the school or college. This breaks away from the traditional 'instinctive' approach, but is far more dependable and practical than an emotional or pragmatic response to services, and helps promote the image of librarians as managers, able to assume managerial responsibility.

Within this area of service measurement, three dimensions are clear. These are concerned with the effectiveness of a service, its costs in relation to its effectiveness, and the relationships between the cost of a service and any perceived or measured benefits to its users. The ways of carrying out methods of measurement vary enormously and, particularly in the educational environment, some benefits cannot be easily labelled or measured. It is possible to some extent to determine the success of user demands in the educational context by looking at the ways in which the demands of specialist groups of users are satisfied, such as part-time students, research students and teaching staff. Their views can contribute to an assessment of library performance, and the librarian has a clearly defined set of users and relatively well defined set of needs to plan for.

However, it is possible to use in schools and colleges some of the methods used in the public and special library sectors, such as checking the availability of specific materials, the speed of answering queries, using questionnaires, data collection and seminars. There is a considerable literature on the subject, including the self-assessment type of manuals from the USA, and also an increasing number of courses dealing with the problem. As well as reference and lending functions, including the provision and availability of text books, the use of on-line services and increasingly sophisticated equipment needs to be considered. The compilation of relatively 'simple' records, such as issues, are very crude tools in this increasingly sophisticated process, but it is important for schools and colleges to make their contribution to the measurement of services. The bibliography includes some texts which can be used as guidelines, but for the busy school or college librarian it may be helpful either to utilise the research department of his or her own Authority, or to take part in locally initiated schemes based in the education sector. These will help to provide useful information, will be based on sound methodology, and will probably be more objective than in-house research.

As with any investigative problem, funding, staffing, constraints and mere apathy may hinder progress, but if evaluation forms part of the long-term planning process, a more realistic programme can be offered to pupils and students. It is crucial to understand the needs and aspirations of the clientèle served by a library, so that the services can reflect these.

Information — a selective list of relevant groups, institutes and associations

British Educational Research
Association
P. Chambers
c/o Bradford College
Great Horton Road
Bradford BD7 1AY

British Library
Information Officer for User
Education
Loughborough University of
Technology
Loughborough
Leics. LE11 3TU

British Library
Research and Development
Department
3 Sheraton Street
London W1V 4BH

Centre for Applied Research in
Education
University of East Anglia
Norwich

Centre for Library and Information
Management
Loughborough University
Loughborough
Leics. LE11 3TU

Centre for Research on User Studies
(CRUS)
University of Sheffield
Western Bank
Sheffield S10 2TN

Council for Educational Technology
(CET)
3 Devonshire Street
London W1N 2BA

Department of Education and
Science
(Assessment of Performance Unit)
Elizabeth House
York Road
London SE1 7PH

Inner London Education Authority (ILEA)
Research and Statistics Department
Addington Street Annexe
London SE1

Library and Information Research
Group
c/o Ian Malley
The Library
Loughborough University of
Technology
Loughborough
Leics. LE11 3TU

Local Government O.R. Unit
201 Kings Road
Reading RG1 4LH

National Association of Inspectors
and Educational Advisers (NAIEA)
Manor Farm House
Preston New Road
Samlesbury
Preston PR5 0UP

National Council for Educational
Standards
1 Hinchley Way
Esher
Surrey KT10 0BD

National Foundation for Educational
Research (NFER)
The Mere
Upton Park
Slough
Berks. SL1 2DQ

219

Office of Management Studies
Association of Research Libraries
1527 New Hampshire Avenue NW
Washington DC 20036
USA

Open University (OU)
Milton Keynes
MK7 6AA

Schools Council
160 Great Portland Street
London W1N 6LL

Society for Research into Higher
Education Ltd
University of Surrey
Guildford
Surrey GU2 5XH

● Journals — a selective list

Aslib Information
Aslib
3 Belgrave Square
London SW1X 8PL

CRUS News
Centre for Research on User Studies
University of Sheffield
Western Bank
Sheffield S10 2TN

*Current Research in Library and
Information Science*
Library Association
7 Ridgmount Street
London WC1E 7AE

Evaluation Newsletter
Society for Research into Higher
Education Ltd
University of Surrey
Guildford
Surrey GU2 5XH

Infuse
British Library
Information Officer for User
Education
Loughborough University of
Technology
Loughborough
Leics. LE11 3TU

*Journal of Applied Educational
Studies*
c/o 6 Fircroft Court
Gerrards Cross Road
Stoke Poges
Bucks.

Journal of Evaluation in Education
7 Ledward Lane
Bowdon
Cheshire WA14

Journal of the NAIEA
Manor Farm House
Preston New Road
Samlesbury
Preston PR5 0UP

*Library and Information Research
News*
c/o Ian Malley
The Library
Loughborough University of
Technology
Loughborough
Leics. LE11 3TU

*Library and Information Science
Abstracts (LISA)*
Library Association
7 Ridgmount Street
London WC1E 7AE

Schools Council Newsletter
Schools Council
160 Great Portland Street
London W1N 6LL

Schools Council Record of
Achievement Newsletter
Schools Council
160 Great Portland Street
London W1N 6LL

Social Science Information Studies
Butterworth
Borough Green
Sevenoaks
Kent

Studies in Higher Education
Carfax Publishing Company
Haddon House
Dorchester-on-Thames
Oxon OX9 8JZ

Teaching at a Distance
Open University
Milton Keynes
MK7 6AA

Where
Advisory Centre for Education (ACE)
18 Victoria Park Square
London E2

● **References — a selective list of books, reports and articles**

Balogh, J. *Profile reports for school leavers.* London, Schools Council, 1982.
Bates, T. and Gallagher, M. (eds) *Formative evaluation of educational television programmes.* London, CET, 1978 (Seminar and conference report 3).
Becher, T., Erant, M. and Knight, J. *Policies for educational accountability.* London, Heinemann Educational, 1982.
Brand, H. *Evaluation, INSET and the teachers centre.* Sheffield City Polytechnic, Department of Education Management, nd.
Burgess, T. and Adams, E. *Outcomes of education.* London, Macmillan, 1980.
Carpenter, R. L. *Statistical methods for librarians.* Chicago, American Library Association, 1978.
Clark, D., Harris, C. G. S., Taylor, P. J., Douglas, A. and Lacey, S. M. J. *The travelling workshops experiment in library user education.* London, British Library Research and Development, 1981 (Report no. 5602).
Coombe Lodge Report *15* No. 1, 1982. *Course evaluation and review: the impact on college structures.* Coombe Lodge, Further Education Staff College, 1982.
Cronin, B. *Self-evaluation guidelines for special libraries: a review of possibilities.* London, Aslib, 1981.
Department of Education and Science. *Aspects of secondary education in England: a survey by HM Inspectors of schools.* London, HMSO, 1979.
Department of Education and Science. *Education in schools — a consultative document.* London, HMSO (Cmnd 6889).
Department of Education and Science. *Local authority arrangements for the school curriculum.* London, HMSO, 1979.

Elliott, G. *Self-evaluation and the teacher: an annotated bibliography and report on current practice 1980, parts 1 and 2.* Hull, University of Hull, London Schools Council, 1980 and 1981.

Elliott, G. 'Self-evaluation and the teacher — a national map' in *Journal of the NAIEA,* No. 14, Spring 1981, pp. 2-5.

Elliott, J. and others. *The SSRC Cambridge Accountability Project.* London, Grant McIntyre, 1982.

Evaluation case study no. 1 (Overhead projector transparencies.) London, National Audio-Visual Aids Library, 1975.

Fjallbrant, N. 'Evaluation in a user education programme' in *Journal of Librarianship,* 9(2), April 1977, pp. 83-95.

Francis, G. M. *A manual for the evaluation of current awareness bulletins.* Boston Spa, British Library, Lending Division, 1981.

Further Education Curriculum Research and Development Unit. *Profiles.* London, FECRADU, 1982.

Haile, B. 'Assessment within school' in *Journal of the NAIEA,* No. 14, Spring 1981, pp. 11-12.

Hamilton, D. F., Jenkins, D. and others. (eds) *Beyond the numbers game: a reader in educational evaluation.* London, Macmillan, 1976.

Harris, C. 'Illuminative evaluation of user education programmes' in *Aslib Proceedings,* 29, 1977, pp. 348-62.

Harris, C. *The travelling workshops experiment: an attempt at 'illuminative evaluation'.* Social Science Information Studies, 1, 1981, pp. 247-253.

Harris, N. D. C. and Bailey, J. D. *Evaluation resource pack.* London, CET, 1981.

Harris, N. D. C., Bell, C. D. and Carter, J. E. H. *Signposts for evaluating: a resource pack.* London, CET, 1981.

Hodges, L. *Out in the open? The schools record debate.* London, Readers and Writers Cooperative, 1982.

ILEA Inspectorate. *Keeping the school under review.* London, ILEA, 1977.

Lancaster, F.W. *Guidelines for the evaluation of information systems and services.* Paris, UNESCO, 1978.

Lawton, D. *The politics of the school curriculum.* London, Routledge and Kegan Paul, 1980.

Line, M. *Library surveys: an introduction to the use, planning procedure and presentation of surveys.* Rev. ed. London, Bingley, 1982.

Lubans, J. *Progress in educating the library user.* London, New York, Bowker, 1979.

Macdonald, B. and Walker, R. (eds) *Innovation, evaluation, research and the problem of control: some interim papers.* Norwich University of East Anglia, Centre for Advanced Research in Education, 1974.

McGormick, R. (ed.) *Calling education to account.* London, Heinemann, 1982.

Malley, I. and Fjallbrant, N. *User education in libraries.* London, Bingley, 1983.

Mansell, J. 'Profiling must be a better way' in *Education,* 29.5.81. *157* (pt 22) p.

479.

Mortimore, P. 'Assessment: time for a change' in *Journal of the NAIEA* No. 14, Spring 1981, pp. 7-10.

Parlett, M. and Dearden, G. (eds) *Introduction to illuminative evaluation: studies in higher education.* Guildford, Society for Research into Higher Education, 1981.

Parlett, M. and Hamilton, D. *'Evaluation as illumination'* in Tawney, D. (ed.) *Curriculum evaluation today: trends and implications* London, Macmillan Educational, 1976.

Rowntree, D. *Assessing students: how shall we know them?* London, Harper and Row, 1979.

Shipman, M. *The limitations of social research.* London, Longman, 1972.

The staff meeting. London, CET, 1975. (Audio tape) (Evaluation case study No. 2).

Shipman, M., Bolan, D. and Jenkins, D. *Inside a curriculum project.* London, Methuen, 1974.

Stake, R. 'The countenance of educational evaluation' in *Teachers College Record, 68,* 1967 (pt 7) pp. 523-40.

Stenhouse, L. *An introduction to curriculum research and development.* London, Heinemann Educational, 1978.

Stenhouse, L. 'Using case study in library research' in *Social science information studies, 1,* 1981, pp. 221-230.

Stevenson, M.B. *User education programmes: a study of their development, organisation, methods and assessment.* London, British Library, 1977 (Research and Development Report No. 5320HC).

Swales, T. *Record of personal achievement: an independent evaluation of the Swindon RPA Scheme.* London, Schools Council, 1980. (Schools Council pamphlet no. 16).

Tawney, D. *Curriculum evaluation today: trends and implications.* London, Macmillan Education, 1976 (Schools Council Research Studies).

Taylor, P.J. 'User education and the role of evaluation' in *Unesco Bulletin for Libraries, XXXII,* (4) July–August 1978, pp. 252-259.

Trow, M. 'Methodological problems in the evaluation of innovations' in Wittrock, M.C. and Wiley, D.E. (eds) *Problems in the evaluation of instruction.* New York, Holt, Rinehart, 1970.

Werking, R.H. 'Evaluating bibliographic education: a review and critique' in *Library Trends,* 1980, pp. 153-192.

Wessel, C.J. 'Criteria for evaluating technical library effectiveness' in *Aslib Proceedings, 20,* (11) 1968, pp. 455-481.

Williams, N. (ed.) *An introduction to evaluation: some notes for schools Council Evaluators.* London, Schools Council, 1979.

Planning pointers

- Help form groups of interested and concerned teachers — these can develop and grow into working parties.

- Involve teachers in these groups in discussions on the use of resources and possible methods of evaluation, within school contexts of curriculum development.

- Keep records/diaries — these contribute to planning and development.

- Attend relevant in-service training and participate with those concerned with data, handling, statistics, and any other methods of evaluation.

- Involve pupils — do not underestimate their opinions — they are the consumers.

- Utilise all expertise available, both in the school and locally.

13　Copyright

There are clear regulations regarding the copyright of print materials, and information and advice on these can be obtained from any of the organisations quoted at the end of this section. The whole area is complex and even more so where the field of non-book materials and music is concerned. The major problems which relate to any of these materials are those of access and control — it is easy to borrow materials and, once borrowed, there is very little or no control over their use and their copying. The same problems apply to other materials, such as video and other commercially produced materials.

The main problem areas relate to music and the performing arts (although these are not of immediate relevance to schools) and the educational world. The infringement of copyright as part of the average school or college day is an established fact, and the Whitford report (*Copyright and design law* 1977) attempted to rationalise the situation through the imposition of a 'blanket' licence agreement, but this has yet to be implemented.

In broad terms, schools and colleges should always check existing regulations (including those involving the Open University), and if in doubt, consult an expert.

●   **Information — a selective list of relevant groups, institutes and associations**

Aslib
3 Belgrave Square
London SW1X 8PL

British Copyright Council
29-33 Berners Street
London W1P 4AA

British Videogram Association Ltd
10 Maddox Street
London W1R 9N

Council for Educational Technology
(CET)
3 Devonshire Street
London W1N 2BA

Library Association
7 Ridgmount Street
London WC1E 7AE

●   **Journals — a selective list**

Aslib Information
Aslib
3 Belgrave Square
London SW1X 8PL

Aslib Proceedings
Aslib
3 Belgrave Square
London SW1X 8PL

Audiovisual Librarian
Library Association Publishing
7 Ridgmount Street
London WC1E 7AE

CET News
CET
3 Devonshire Street
London W1N 2BA

*Library and Information Research
News*
c/o The Library
Hatfield Polytechnic
P.O. Box 110
Hatfield
Herts. AL10 9AD

*Library and Information Services
Abstracts*
Library Association
7 Ridgmount Street
London WC1E 7AE

Library Association Record (LAR)
Library Association
7 Ridgmount Street
London WC1E 7AE

●   **References — a selective list of relevant books, reports and articles**

Copyright and design law: report of the Committee to consider the law on copyright and designs. London, HMSO, 1977. Cmnd 6732. (Whitford Report.)
Copyright and education: the Council's working group on rights. London, CET, 1974 (Working paper 8).
Crabb, G. *Copyright agreement between employees and staff in education.*

London, CET, 1979.

Crabb, G. *Copyright and computers.* London, CET, nd.

Crabb, G. *Copyright and the copying of film.* London, CET, nd.

Crabb, G. *Copyright and the copying of sound recordings for educational purposes.* London, CET, nd.

Crabb, G. *Copyright clearance, a practical guide.* 2nd ed. London, CET, 1981.

Crabb, G. *Off-air recordings of broadcast programmes for educational purposes.* London, CET, nd.

Crabb, G. *Protection of computer programmes.* London, CET, nd.

Crabb, G. *The use of copyright printed material for educational purposes.* London, CET, nd.

Herbert, F. and Noel, W. *Copyright and materials for the handicapped.* Toronto, Canadian National Institute for the Blind, 1982.

Photocopying and the law: a guide for librarians and teachers and other suppliers and users of photocopies of copyright works. London, British Copyright Council, 1970. (Rev. ed. of pamphlet issued by Society of Authors and Publishers Association.)

Plowman, E. W. and Hamilton, C. C. *Copyright: intellectual property in the information age.* London, Routledge & Kegan Paul, 1980.

Reform of the law relating to copyright, designs and performers' protection: a consultative document. London, HMSO, 1981. Cmnd 8302. (The Green Paper.)

Taylor, L. J. *Copyright for librarians.* Hastings, Tamarisk Books, 1980.

Videogram rights. British Videogram Association, 1982.

Abbreviations

AACR2	Anglo American Cataloguing Rules
ACACE	Advisory Council for Adult and Continuing Education
ACE	Advisory Centre for Education
ACFHE	Association of Colleges of Further and Higher Education
ARE	Association for Recurrent Education
ARLIS	Arts Libraries Association
ATCAL	Association for the Teaching of African and Caribbean Literature
ASLIB	Association of Special Libraries and Information Bureaux
AUCBE	Advisory Unit for Computer Based Education
BACIE	British Association for Commercial and Industrial Education
BEC	Business Education Council *now* Business and Technician Education Council
BEI	British Education Index
BHI	British Humanities Index
BIRS	British Institute of Recorded Sound
BLAISE	British Library Automated Information Service
BLCMP	Birmingham Libraries Co-operative Marc Project
C&G	City and Guilds of London Institute
CAB	Citizens Advice Bureau
CAI	Computer Assisted Instruction
CAL	Computer Assisted Learning
CARM	Campaign Against Racism in the Media
CAT	Computer assisted technology
CBI	Confederation of British Industry
CEDAR	Computers in Education as a Resource
CEE	Certificate of Extended Education
CET	Council for Educational Technology
CGLI	City and Guilds of London Institute
CIPFA	Chartered Institute of Public Finance and Accountancy
CLAIM	Centre for Library and Information Management
CLRS	Central Library Resources Service (ILEA)
CML	Computer Managed Learning
CNAA	Council for National Academic Awards
COFHE	Colleges of Further and Higher Education Group (Library Association)

COIC	Careers and Occupational Information Centre
CRE	Commission for Racial Equality
CRUS	Centre for Research on User Studies
DES	Department of Education and Science
DipHe	Diploma in Higher Education
ERIC	Educational Resources Information Centre
FE	Further Education
FECRADU	Further Education Curriculum Review and Development Unit *now* Further Education Unit
IFLA	International Federation of Library Associations
ITB	Industrial Training Board
INSCRU	Information Skills in the Curriculum Research Unit
LAR	Library Association Record
LISA	Library and Information Science Abstracts
LOCAS	Local cataloguing service (British Library)
MARC	Machine Readable Cataloguing
MEP	Microelectronics Education Programme
MSC	Manpower Services Commission
NAME	National Association for Multi Racial Education
NATFHE	National Association of Teachers in Further and Higher Education
NFER	National Foundation for Educational Research
NRCD	National Reprographic Centre for Documentation
NEC	National Extension College
NOP	New Opportunity Courses
NUT	National Union of Teachers
OCLC	Online Computer Library Centre
OLS	Open Learning Systems
OU	Open University
PETRAS	Polytechnic Educational Technology Resources Advisory Service
Rosla	Raising of the school leaving age
RSA	Royal Society of Arts
SEFT	Society for Education in Film and Television
SLG	School Libraries Group (Library Association)
SOCCS	Study of Cataloguing Computer Software
SCOLCAP	Scottish Libraries Co-operative Automation Project
SOAS	School of Oriental and African Studies
SWALCAP	South West Academic Libraries Co-operative Project
TEC	Technician Education Council *now* Business and Technician Education Council
TOPS	Training Opportunities Programme (MSC)
TUC	Trades Union Congress

USPECS	User Specifications (CET)
UVP	Unified Vocational Preparation
VIC	Video Interface with computers
WEA	Workers Educational Association
YOP	Youth Opportunities Scheme (MSC)

Index